D0332400

H46 373 511 5

TECHNOLOGY

TECHN

LARGE HADRON COLLIDER (SEE PAGES 32–33)

OLOGY

CLIVE GIFFORD

SCHOLASTIC discover more™

How to discover more

This book is simple to use and enjoy, but knowing a little bit about how it works will help you discover more about technology. Have a great read!

How the pages work
The book is divided into chapters, such as **Microchips & smart tech**. Each chapter is made up of stand-alone spreads (double pages) that focus on specific topics.

Timeline spreads
Timeline spreads (pages 24–25, 44–45, 68–69, and 92–93) give you the most important dates and events in the history of technological inventions.

Fact boxes
Some spreads include a profile box with details about a specific invention.

Fantastic facts
BIG text gives an amazing fact or quote!

Step-by-step
Look out for picture sequences that show every step in a process.

How robots work [Nuts and bolts]

Robots are machines that perform difficult, repetitive, or dangerous tasks for us. Most robots gather information about their surroundings using cameras and other sensors. They then follow instructions given by an onboard computer or sent by remote control.

PackBot specifications	
Made by	iRobot, USA
Introduced	2002
Length (minus flippers)	68.6 cm (27 ins)
Width	40.6 cm (16 ins)
Height (arm retracted)	17.8 cm (7 ins)
Weight (minus batteries)	20.4 kg (45 lbs)
Power	2 lithium-ion batteries
Sensors	Accelerometers, compass, GPS, cameras, inclinometer
Top speed	9.3 kph (5.8 mph)

PackBot
A human operator controls this mobile robot from a distance by remote control. PackBot can detect and disarm bombs, handle dangerous chemicals, and even explore damaged nuclear power stations.

PackBot in action
With its surveillance camera, a PackBot peers into a van thought to contain a bomb.

Multipurpose roving robot
As PackBot moves, it communicates with its controller. It can carry out a range of tasks using arm tools, called end effectors.

Surveillance camera
This colour camera can magnify up to 312 times.

LED array
Bright light-emitting diode (LED) lamps illuminate the scene viewed by the camera.

Gripper
This gripper is just one of PackBot's range of arm tools.

Extendable arm
Able to lift 13.6 kg (30 lbs), the arm can also turn and work around corners.

Controller
A microprocessor in the body coordinates the robot's actions.

Drive camera
This shows the route ahead, and tilts to give a close view of the gripper.

Rotating flippers

Rounded track belts
Tracks enable PackBot to tackle mud, snow, and steep slopes.

90: the number of seconds it takes to get **PackBot** up and running

Other PackBot arm tools

FLASHLIGHT | CABLE CUTTER | GLASS BREAKER | ROUTE CLEARANCE TOOL KIT

Tracks and flippers
Mobile robots with legs or with tanklike tracks are better at crossing rough ground than wheeled machines are. PackBot's tracks and movable flippers enable the robot to overcome obstacles in its path.

The flippers tilt, and their tracks grip the ground

Rotating flippers haul the robot over the ridge

The flippers rotate until they face ahead again.

1 Climbing a ridge
When PackBot reaches the top of a ridge or a sharp dip, the flippers tilt down.

2 Over the top
The flippers then move back and underneath the robot, propelling it forwards.

3 Straight ahead
Having overcome the obstacle, PackBot trundles off at up to 2.6 m (8.5 ft) per second.

Digital companion book

Download your free, all-new digital book:

Cool Tech Heroes

Log on to
www.scholastic.com/discovermore

Enter your unique code:
RXP29TGPD42R

Shigeru Miyamoto [Video game creator]

Japanese video game designer Shigeru Miyamoto has dreamed up some of the most exciting and successful video games of all time, including Donkey Kong (1981), which was one of the first-ever video games sold for consoles at home. At the time, video games were mostly played on huge machines at arcades. Miyamoto also created the Super Mario Bros. video games, which are the bestselling games in the world. He is also credited with encouraging the development of Nintendo's Wii system.

Video game footage   Shigeru Miyamoto

A Wii games system

Most modern games

Miyamoto Bio Box

220 million
Super Mario video games have been sold since 1985

Discover more about video game consoles

Discover all about the people who created cool technologies.

Shigeru Miyan

Born: 16 November 1952, in Sonobe, Kyoto, Japan
College: 1970–1975, Kanazawa Municipal College of Industrial

Career highlights

1980   1981   1983

Mario Bros.

Sheriff, Nintendo

Donkey Kong

2010–11   2005

The Wall of Game

Super Mario

GameCube

Click the pop-ups for extra stories.

More here columns
This feature suggests books to read, places to visit, things to do, and keywords to learn.

Spread types

Look out for different kinds of spreads such as stats spreads and photographic spreads. Other spreads explode an amazing technology so you can see everything inside.

LOOK-INSIDE SPREAD

A look-inside spread pulls apart a familiar object and explores the different technologies that combine to make it work efficiently.

STATS SPREAD

A stats spread is packed full of facts, amazing statistics, and fun infographics.

Robot thinking
Some robots can work on their own, but they must still be programmed beforehand by humans. Massive advances in programming, computing, and sensors will be necessary before robots can be truly intelligent and able to think for themselves.

Artificial intelligence?
Sci-fi films, such as *I, Robot* (2004), often feature free-thinking robots, but that technology is still a long way off.

Radio transmitter
Data and audio signals are relayed via the radio transmitter

Communications cable
Cable played out by this spool links the robot with its operator

36/37
MICROCHIPS & SMART TECH

More here

robotics end effector
sensors hazmat robots
mobile robots
robot controllers

Robot Adventures with Robosapien™ and Friends: Introduction to Robotics (Vision One Pictures, 2010)

Go to one of the events held for National Robotics Week every April (www.nationalroboticsweek.org).

Visit the robotics collection at the Massachusetts Institute of Technology Museum, Cambridge, Massachusetts, USA.

accelerometer: a sensor that detects and measures movement (see page 47).
autonomous: self-controlling. Autonomous robots can work without human supervision.
inclinometer: a sensor that can measure the angles of slopes.
sensor: a device that can detect (and sometimes measure) aspects of its surroundings, such as heat, light, and movement.

Key to symbols in More here columns

Suggested reading

Keywords for web searches

Fact file

Places to visit

Mini glossary

Watch

Mini-glossary
This explains challenging words and phrases found on the spread.

PHOTOGRAPHIC SPREAD

This type of spread focuses on an extraordinary subject, often providing an unfamiliar view, such as these thrill-seekers on a rollercoaster.

Glossary and index

The glossary explains words and phrases that might not be explained fully on the spreads or in the **More here** columns. The index can help you find pages throughout the book on which words and topics appear.

Read in-depth technology encyclopedia entries.

Look up technology words.

Project editor: Steve Setford
Project art editor: Mark Lloyd
Designer: Clare Joyce
Art director: Bryn Walls
Managing editor: Miranda Smith
Cover design: Natalie Godwin
DTP: John Goldsmid
Visual content editor: Dwayne Howard
Executive Director of Photography,
Scholastic: Steve Diamond

"Any...advanced technology is indistinguishable from magic."
—ARTHUR C. CLARKE, 1961

Copyright © 2012 Scholastic Inc

All rights reserved. Published by Scholastic Inc., *Publishers since
1920.* SCHOLASTIC, SCHOLASTIC DISCOVER MORE ™, and associated logos
are trademarks and/or registered trademarks of Scholastic Inc.

No part of this publication may be reproduced, stored in a retrieval
system, or transmitted in any form or by any means, electronic,
mechanical, photocopying, recording, or otherwise, without the
written permission of the publisher. For information regarding
permission, please write to Scholastic Inc., Attention: Permissions
Department, 557 Broadway, New York, NY 10012.

Library of Congress Cataloging-in-Publication Data Available
Distributed in the UK by Scholastic UK Ltd, Westfield Road, Southam,
Warwickshire, England CV47 0RA

ISBN 978-1-407-13156-6

10 9 8 7 6 5 4 3 2 1   12 13 14 15 16

Printed in Singapore   46
First edition, May 2012

Scholastic is constantly working to lessen the environmental impact of our
manufacturing processes. To view our industry- leading paper procurement
policy, visit www.scholastic.com/ paperpolicy.

Contents

Ant's head in close-up

Technology has helped people examine objects that are impossible to see with the naked eye. This image was made by a powerful, high-tech microscope that moves a beam of electrons across a tiny object, such as an ant's head. An incredibly detailed image is created from the patterns of electrons scattered by the object.

New Mars rover

Curiosity, a robotic vehicle, is tested by scientists in Pasadena, California, USA. In 2012, after travelling 77 million km (48 million miles) through space, Curiosity will look for signs of life on Mars. Since the space programme began, scientists have developed technologies to investigate our solar system and the Universe beyond it.

510 LBS

Micro
& sma

* What's so smart about smartphones?

* How can technology help you when you're lost?

* Why do robots play soccer?

chips
rt tech

Shrinking tech [Smaller...

In the history of technology, progress sometimes means building bigger and stronger. But many recent advances involve packing more abilities and functions into smaller and smaller spaces.

Martin Cooper
In 1973, a team at Motorola led by Martin Cooper invented the first handheld mobile. Their prototype device was the forerunner of the DynaTAC (see left).

Phone revolution
Early portable phones resembled walkie-talkies, but they were bulky and heavy. To make them easy to carry, batteries and electronic components had to be shrunk in size.

Pye mobile, 1972
This shoulder-worn device was one of the earliest mobile phones. It made calls by dialling into telephone systems.

Car phone, 1982
The Nokia Mobira Senator, the first portable car phone, had its own battery pack so that it could be carried around. It weighed a hefty 9.8 kg (22 lb)!

A mobile revolution
The invention of transistors (see next page) helped usher in smaller and more powerful devices such as portable transistor radios and, from the 1980s onwards, mobile phones. As more and more transistors have been shrunk onto microchips, so mobile phones have shrunk in size and boomed in power. Today's mobiles come with many built-in features.

1983

Name	Motorola DynaTAC 8000X
Weight	794 g (28 oz)
Cool fact	The first handheld mobile phone to go on sale

Expensive pioneer
Standing over 33 cm (13 in) tall and with a battery that allowed just 30–60 minutes of talk time, the pioneering 8000X cost an astonishing $3,995.

1989

Name	Motorola MicroTAC
Weight	349 g (12.3 oz)
Cool fact	The first mobile phone with a flip-down format

Flip-down first
The MicroTAC was smaller than earlier phones, with a flap that folded down to show its keypad. The screen could display just eight characters.

865.7 million:
the number of mobile phone users in India in August 2011

Smaller and smaller

Valves, or vacuum tubes, were used as switches or amplifiers in early radios and computers. They were replaced by small transistors in the 1950s. Microchips began to replace transistors in the 1970s.

VALVE   **TRANSISTOR**   **MICROCHIP**

From valve to microchip
Many millions of transistors can be etched on a single tiny microchip – a fraction of the size of a valve – to provide phenomenal computing power.

1996

Name	Motorola StarTAC
Weight	88 g (3.1 oz)
Cool fact	One of the first phones with lithium-ion batteries

Good vibrations
The smallest, lightest phone at the time, the StarTAC was also the first mobile phone that could vibrate as well as ring when it received calls.

2002

Name	BlackBerry 5810
Weight	133 g (4.7 oz)
Cool fact	The first BlackBerry email/phone device

Surfer's phone
You could email and surf the Internet on the 5810, but since it had no built-in microphone or speaker, you had to attach a headset to make voice calls.

2011

Name	LG Optimus 3D
Weight	168 g (5.93 oz)
Cool fact	The first phone with a glasses-free 3D display

3D marvel
Two 5-megapixel cameras produce images that merge into a 3D view on the Optimus' display. It also has Wi-Fi and 8GB of memory.

Powerful processor

A computer's microprocessor sits on top
of its motherboard – the circuit board that
links it to the rest of the computer. The
microprocessor, or central processing unit
(CPU), is the "brain" that controls most
of the computer's functions. It consists
of a complex arrangement of transistors
(see page 15). Some microprocessors can
contain up to 2.6 billion transistors!

Thousands or millions of transistors (see page 15), working together, enable a personal computer (PC) to perform complex calculations incredibly rapidly. PCs work with digital data – a flow of 1s or 0s, each stored as a binary digit (or bit) of memory. This data is represented as an on-or-off flow of electric signals inside a computer's circuits.

Analogue and digital

PCs can only use digital data, but much information, such as sound waves, is continuous and varying. This analogue data must be sampled and converted into digital data – a series of 1s and 0s that represents the original analogue information.

Wavelike analogue signal

LEVEL

0000000011111110000111
0011111100111001111000
1101000010001000100010

TIME

Converting to digital
An analogue-to-digital converter takes small samples of an analogue signal and gives a precise number to each sample.

Digital signal
Each digital sample has a precise value in terms of 1s and 0s.

RAM chips
Together, these chips provide the computer with 4GB of RAM (see next page).

Hard-disk drive
This drive stores 750GB of data on magnetic disks, which spin up to 7,400 times per minute.

325
million PCs were sold worldwide in 2010

Aluminium unibody
The case is made from a single sheet of aluminium metal that is bent, shaped, and cut.

Inside your computer

A PC, like this MacBook Pro i7 laptop, contains many physical components, called hardware. Together with instructions called programs, or software, they enable the computer to store and process digital data. A group of programs called an operating system controls its basic functions.

Airport card
A circuit board and antenna make Bluetooth and Wi-Fi connections.

Superdrive
This can play DVDs and CDs, and record onto blank disks.

Name	Apple I
Introduced	1976
Cool fact	Sold in kit form; 4KB of RAM

Name	Apple MacBook Air
Introduced	2008
Cool fact	Half a million times the memory of the Apple I

PC evolution

Early PCs had no sound or graphics, and limited memory capacity. Data was stored on punched cards or magnetic tape. Modern PCs have many thousands of times more processing power.

Cooling fan
Two fans cool the components to keep them from overheating.

Motherboard
This circuit board holds many of the PC's core components (see right).

The vital parts

The diagram below shows the interaction of the key components involved in handling and storing data and running programs, such as the central processing unit (CPU) and several different types of memory.

Control unit
The CPU's control unit receives and carries out instructions from the memory.

Arithmetic logic unit (ALU)
The ALU, also part of the CPU, performs calculations requested by the control unit.

MOTHERBOARD

Registers
These are small-capacity memory banks within the CPU that it can access directly.

CONTROL · ALU

INPUT · REGISTERS · OUTPUT

CPU

ROM · RAM

Read-only memory (ROM)
The ROM is permanent storage for data that does not change or get erased when the PC is switched off. It holds vital instructions, called firmware, that enable the machine to work.

Central processing unit (CPU)
The CPU controls most of the computer's functions and directs the flow of data.

Random-access memory (RAM)
The CPU uses the RAM to temporarily store data on which it is working.

Rechargeable battery
Making up about 20 per cent of the laptop's weight, the battery can power up to seven hours of use.

STORAGE

Storage
A set of memory chips or a hard-disk drive holds programs and the user's personal data.

Smartphone [Power at your

A smartphone is a small computer in the form of a mobile phone. Able to handle phone calls, texts, and emails, smartphones go way beyond the basics with programs called apps (see page 23), which enable users to perform hundreds of different tasks.

225 million: the number of touches a touchscreen is built to take

What's inside?

A smartphone contains a computing system on a microprocessor, memory, and devices to handle its graphics, sounds, and display. A program called an operating system – such as Android, Symbian, or Apple iOS – controls the phone's operation.

Pocket power
A smartphone has more memory and processing power than a personal computer from the 1990s had.

Touchscreen technology

Some smartphones include a small physical keyboard, but most have a touchscreen. This displays icons and scroll bars. Users touch or swipe these to enter information and commands.

Capacitive layer
Current flowing through this grid creates an electric field across the screen.

Sensing layer
Vertical and horizontal sensor lines detect changes to the electric field.

Glass visual display
Displays are typically 7.6–11.4 cm (3–4.5 ins) across diagonally.

Screen coating
A scratch-resistant coating also reduces reflections, to make the display easier to read in bright light.

3 Disturbed field
The transfer of charge disturbs the electric field on the capacitive layer.

2 Finger touch
When the user touches the screen, charge transfers to the finger.

4 Sensors
The change in the electric field is measured by sensors.

Exploded phone
A smartphone is packed full of parts, and even its screen consists of several different layers. As many as 2,000 individual components have to fit into its slim casing, which is often made of tough, lightweight plastic.

1 Screen charge
A small electric charge is applied to the screen from all four corners.

Capacitive screen
Many touchscreens use a capacitive system, which detects changes to an electric field caused by the touch of a finger.

5 Alerting controller
The sensors send data to the screen's controller, which calculates where on the screen the touch occurred.

fingertips]

Removable storage card
A microSD (Secure Digital) card lets the user transfer data and photos to and from computers.

Speaker
Sounds are broadcast to the user's ear.

SIM card
The Subscriber Identity Module (SIM) memory chip stores phone numbers and other personal information.

Digital camera
Photos taken by the user can be stored in the memory and sent to other people.

Microprocessor
A powerful processor is the smartphone's computing centre.

Image and video processor chip
This allows the phone to play videos on its display.

Lithium-ion battery
(See box below.)

Lightweight casing

Wi-Fi transmitter and receiver
The phone can access the Internet whenever a Wi-Fi hotspot is nearby.

Microphone
The user's voice is changed into electrical signals.

RAM chip
The operating system is stored on a Random Access Memory (RAM) chip.

Metal shield
This protects the electronic parts.

Lithium-ion battery

Recharging a phone's flat battery causes all its ions (electrically charged lithium atoms) to move from the positive terminal to the negative terminal. When the phone is used, the ions flow in the opposite direction, from negative to positive.

Negative terminal

Positive terminal

Lithium ions

Electron flow

Electricity supply

Ions move to negative terminal

Ions move to positive terminal

Electron flow

Phone

1 No charge
With all the ions at the positive terminal, the battery is flat and can provide no power.

2 Charging
The ions begin to flow when the phone is plugged into an electricity supply.

3 Fully charged
With all the ions now at the negative terminal, the battery is ready to use again.

4 In use
Electrons power the phone. Lithium ions flow back to the positive terminal.

Mobile phones work by changing speech, text messages, and images into radio waves. The radio waves travel to their destinations via radio antennae called base stations. When you make a call, you set in motion an amazing sequence of events.

Mobile phone network

A mobile phone network is divided into thousands of areas called cells, each with a base station. A cell's size depends on the number of calls made in that area. Busy city-centre cells are small, because they each have to handle many callers. Cells work in groups of seven, with each group linked to a ground station.

Phoning a friend
The call starts when you dial your friend's number. As you talk, the phone changes your words into electrical signals.

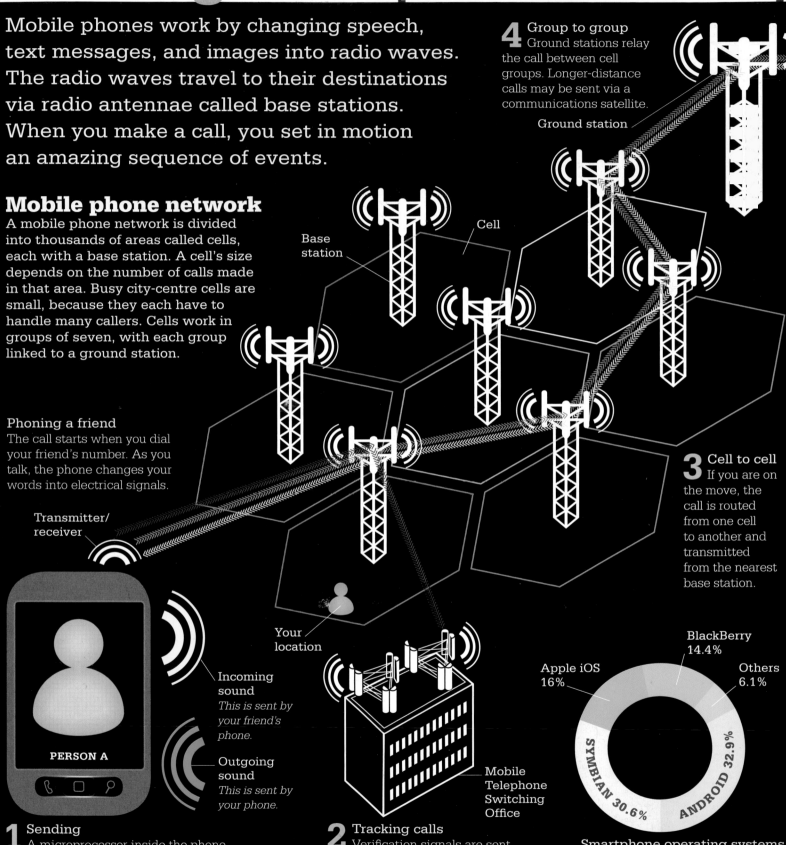

4 Group to group
Ground stations relay the call between cell groups. Longer-distance calls may be sent via a communications satellite.

Ground station

Cell

Base station

Transmitter/ receiver

3 Cell to cell
If you are on the move, the call is routed from one cell to another and transmitted from the nearest base station.

Your location

Incoming sound
This is sent by your friend's phone.

Outgoing sound
This is sent by your phone.

PERSON A

Mobile Telephone Switching Office

BlackBerry 14.4%

Apple iOS 16%

Others 6.1%

SYMBIAN 30.6%

ANDROID 32.9%

1 Sending
A microprocessor inside the phone converts electrical voice signals into digital data. Your phone sends the data as radio waves to a local base station.

2 Tracking calls
Verification signals are sent to a Mobile Telephone Switching Office (MTSO). The MTSO keeps track of the phone's location.

Smartphone operating systems
This shows the four most popular operating systems worldwide at the start of 2011 (see page 20).

5 Destination reached
The call is routed to the cell nearest to your friend. When your friend answers, the reply travels in the opposite direction.

Location of friend

PERSON B

302.6 million
– the number of smartphones sold worldwide during 2010

6 Receiving
Your friend's phone converts the radio signal back into electrical signals, and a speaker broadcasts your voice.

Applications
Apps can be downloaded from the Internet to a smartphone. These small, efficient computer programs give your smartphone extra capabilities. Apple's online iPhone store contains over 500,000 different apps.

Text
Websites, news feeds, and electronic books can be read on-screen with these apps.

Travel
Travel apps may provide tourist information and up-to-date plane and train travel times, or translate foreign languages.

Social networking
Some apps give access to sites such as Facebook, Twitter, and LinkedIn.

Sounds
These apps are for listening to radio stations and music, and making recordings.

Navigation
Some apps use maps and GPS (see pages 30–31) to help you find your way around.

Games
The most popular apps are games, ranging from quizzes and puzzles to action games.

Types of app
Here are some popular types of app. They do not include utilities – apps that improve your phone's performance.

More here

Profiles: Tech Titans by Carla Killough McClafferty

Read the life stories of the founders of Google, the company that developed the Android operating system for smartphones.

Android iOS **apps** augmented reality **IBM Simon** SMS communications satellite

Dallas Museum of Art, Dallas, Texas, USA

Visit one of the first museums to offer a smartphone tour that adds commentary, facts, and images on visitors' smartphones as they view exhibits.

Mobile Telephone Switching Office (MTSO): a computer system that monitors phone calls and their locations, transfers calls between cells, and tracks the length and cost of calls.

short message service (SMS): this allows text messages of up to 160 characters to be sent between mobile phones.

Information technology

The first computers were unreliable machines used only by specially trained technicians to make complex calculations. In little more than 50 years, computers have developed into powerful tools that anyone can use for work, learning, and entertainment.

1971
Microprocessor
The first general purpose computer microprocessor (see pages 16–17) was the Intel 4004. It combined many of the key components of a computer onto a tiny wafer of silicon, called a silicon chip, or microchip.

INTEL 4004
CHIP CASE

1642
Calculator
PASCAL'S MACHINE

A practical mechanical calculator, the Pascaline, was invented by French mathematician Blaise Pascal when he was only 18. It could add up numbers eight digits long.

1943
Colossus, the first programmable electronic computer, was used in England to crack German codes during World War II.

Dots represent 10-year increases.

1956
American computer company IBM introduced its 350 Disk Storage Unit – the first hard-disk drive (see page 18).

1971
In the USA, the first electronic mail (email) message was sent over a computer network by Ray Tomlinson, a computer programmer.

1974
One of the first computers on sale to the public, the Altair 8080, came as a kit and had to be built by the buyer.

1960•   1970•

1946
The Electronic Numerical Integrator and Computer (ENIAC), developed by the US Army, could do more than 5,000 calculations per second.

1963
At California's Stanford University, Douglas Engelbart and Bill English built the first computer mouse.

1834
Mechanical computer
Englishman Charles Babbage designed his analytical engine, a device that would be able to perform a range of mathematical tasks. He never completed it.

ANALYTICAL ENGINE (INCOMPLETE)

1951
UNIVAC I
Costing $1.5 million, UNIVAC I was the first mass-produced, commercially available computer. UNIVAC I stored information on magnetic tape and punched (holed) cards.

13 tonnes:
the weight of a UNIVAC computer in the 1950s

BILL GATES

American pioneer

Founded: Microsoft Corp.

Developed: Windows operating system

1985
Microsoft vs. Apple

Microsoft released its Windows operating system (see page 18), which was used on many PCs. Rival company Apple, which launched its first Macintosh (Mac) computer in 1984, used its own operating system.

STEVE JOBS

American pioneer

Founded: Apple Inc.

Developed: Apple computers, tablets, and iPods

1991
World Wide Web

The web is a vast collection of electronic pages (web pages) that can be viewed on computers via the Internet (see pages 26–29). Devised in 1989, it was first made available to the public in 1991.

AN ARTIST'S IDEA OF THE WEB

1981
The Epson HX-20 – the first laptop-size portable computer – was launched. It was powered by a rechargeable battery

1997
IBM's Deep Blue computer defeated world chess champion Garry Kasparov, 3½–2½, in a six-game series.

1990 • **2000** • **2010**

1996
Universal Serial Bus (USB) connectors, used to link electronic devices to computers, were introduced.

2004
The Facebook social networking site (see page 29) was started by Mark Zuckerberg and his friends.

2005
The YouTube website was launched. The site allows users to share their videos with others online.

2008
Search engine company Google claimed that its database contained at least 1 trillion web pages.

1976
Supercomputer

The Cray-1, the first supercomputer, was built in the USA by Seymour Cray, an electrical engineer. It could make millions of calculations per second but weighed 5 tonnes.

CRAY-1 SUPERCOMPUTER

2010
Apple iPad

The iPad was Apple's first tablet – a hand-held computer with a touchscreen. In terms of size and weight, tablets are between laptops and mobile phones.

APPLE iPAD TABLET

2,507 trillion: the number of calculations per second that China's Tianhe-1 supercomputer can perform

Internet [Spanning the globe]

The Internet is sometimes called the world's biggest machine. In fact, it is millions of machines – computers, routers, and servers (see below) – all linked together with wired and wireless connections. Common rules, called protocols, enable them to work together so that people can send emails, upload and download files, play games against one another online, and view pages from the World Wide Web.

Information highway

Internet data can travel as electrical signals along phone lines, as radio signals relayed by space satellites, or as pulses of light through very thin glass strands inside fibre-optic cables. Most home computers connect to the Internet via a modem.

Home computer and modem
When you click on a link to a webpage on your computer, the modem converts the digital request from your computer into an analogue signal. This signal is sent over a phone, coaxial, or fibre cable as packets of data.

Internet service provider (ISP)
The data packets requesting the webpage arrive at the computers of an ISP, a company that manages your Internet connection. Devices called routers direct your request to the correct destination.

Microsoft data centre
Owned by Microsoft, this building
in Chicago, USA, can house up
to 224,000 servers that operate
24 hours a day, 7 days a week.
In total, data centres consume
around 1.3 percent of the world's
entire electricity supply.

More here

*20 Things I Learned About
Browsers and the Web*
(available for free at
www.20thingsilearned
.com/en-US)

*How Did That Get to
My House?: Internet*
by Gary Chmielewski

computer network
Vinton Cerf **ARPANET**
Tim Berners-Lee
Internet backbone
domain name server

client: in a computer
network, a computer
or device that requests
information.

exabyte: a unit of
information or computer
storage that is equal to
one quintillion bytes.

internet traffic: the
amount of data sent
via the Internet, often
measured per month.

server: a computer that
relays data or resources
to client computers in
a computer network.

Data centre
Internet information, such as the webpage
you want to view, is usually stored at data
centres. These are collections of special
computers called servers, which receive
and respond to requests for information.

Webpage
Your home computer has its own unique
address, called an IP address. Servers and
routers on the Internet use this address
to direct the flow of information – in this
case, a webpage – back to your computer.

80.5:
**the number of
exabytes of Internet
traffic predicted
per month for the
year 2015 (that's
enough to fill
20 billion DVDs)**

Net numbers

Net numbers | What we do

From its humble origins in the 1970s as a computer network linking universities and other large organizations in the United States, the Internet has mushroomed. Today, more than 2 billion people are online with access to the Internet.

Emailing
Electronic mail (email) involves sending text messages over the Internet. Photos, videos, and music files can also be attached to an email. In 2010, over 107 trillion emails were sent – that's more than 3.4 million every second!

Global email
This is how the world's 2.9 billion email accounts are distributed. About a quarter of these are business accounts.

North America 14%

Rest of the world 16%

EUROPE 23%

ASIA / PACIFIC 47%

Surfing
People surfing, or browsing, the World Wide Web (see page 25) can ask search engines to help them find the website or information they want. Google, with over 36,000 requests per second, is the most popular search engine.

Web growth
The number of websites hosted on the World Wide Web has boomed since the web became accessible to the public in 1991.

204
SEPTEMBER 1993

300,000
JULY 1996

255,000,000
JULY 2011

Interlinked world
Through emailing, social networking, gaming, and surfing, the Internet connects people across the globe.

Gaming
Video games can be played online via specialized gaming websites or social networking sites (see opposite page). Some are simple one-player games. Others involve complex graphics, virtual worlds, and thousands or even millions of players competing against one another simultaneously.

55,502,30■

active users played the FarmVille game on Facebook in 2011

Socializing
Social networking websites help people keep in touch with their friends – both old and new – and share their interests with others. They include Facebook, LinkedIn, and Twitter. Facebook is the biggest of them all.

KEY

👤 = 2 MILLION PEOPLE

Top Facebook users
The five countries shown below had the most Facebook members in September 2011.

1 **UNITED STATES** 155,746,780 — **50%** of its population

2 **INDONESIA** 40,420,180 — **17%** of its population

3 **INDIA** 36,421,720 — **3%** of its population

4 **TURKEY** 30,735,100 — **42%** of its population

5 **UNITED KINGDOM** 30,337,440 — **48%** of its population

Shopping
Many companies, such as the online retailer Amazon.com, use websites to sell their products by mail order. Buyers of software, videos, and music can often download products directly to their computers and smartphones.

Online auctions
With more than 6.4 million new items for sale each day, eBay is the largest Internet auction site.

SOLD 2001 $4,900,000 GULFSTREAM II JET Priciest completed sale on eBay

SOLD 2004 £61,000 50,000-YEAR-OLD MAMMOTH SKELETON Strangest completed sale on eBay

Blogging
Short for *web log*, a blog is a personal journal on the World Wide Web. Blogs are updated regularly with the opinions and feelings of the author (the "blogger"). Many have photos and links to websites and other blogs.

170 million: **the number of blogs in September 2011**

Navigation [Help from above]

Originally designed for the US military, the Global Positioning System (GPS) is a network of satellites that helps users on Earth find their location, accurate to within a few metres. It is one of several satellite navigation systems worldwide. Russia's system, GLONASS, became available to the public in 2007, while the European Union's Galileo project is expected to be operational by 2018.

Solar panel
Energy from the Sun's rays powers the satellite.

Fin for tagging
A tag is usually fitted to a shark's dorsal fin. After a set amount of time, the tag detaches itself and rises to the surface.

Satellites above

GPS currently relies on 24 satellites. Each satellite orbits Earth twice each day, continually transmitting its precise location. It also transmits the time, which is calculated by onboard atomic clocks to within billionths of a second.

GPS network
Groups of 4 satellites travel on 6 different orbits. From almost any place on Earth, a GPS receiver can obtain signals from at least 4 of the 24 satellites.

Finding your position
The GPS receiver uses the positions of the satellites in space and the time differences in the arrival of their signals to calculate its own location on Earth.

20,200 km (12,550 miles): the approximate altitude above Earth's surface of each GPS satellite

Satellite signals
Signals from the different satellites arrive within milliseconds of one another.

Person with receiver
The receiver uses the signals to find its location.

Everyday uses

GPS receivers can be integrated into microprocessors (see pages 16–17) and fitted inside many electronic devices. For example, voice-guided GPS systems called "sat navs" give drivers spoken directions to their destinations.

Mapping on the move
A smartphone with a GPS receiver and mapping software can locate the user and show the way to nearby attractions.

Emergency!
By keeping track of their vehicles with GPS, ambulance services can direct the nearest one to the scene of an accident.

At the ends of the Earth
GPS works all over the world. Even polar explorers and scientists can use GPS to navigate in icy, featureless landscapes.

Great white shark
Large marine animals, such as great whites, are often tracked with pop-up tags, which float to the surface and beam signals to an Argos satellite.

Keeping track

A satellite system called Argos allows researchers to track the movements of wild animals. A small tag attached to an animal gathers and stores data. It then sends the data to one of the Argos satellites, which uses radio waves to relay signals back to the researchers.

Great white journey
A tag fitted to a great white shark nicknamed Nicole allowed researchers to map its 99-day journey from the coast of South Africa to Australia. On its long swim, the shark travelled 11,000 kilometres (6,800 miles)!

AFRICA

INDIAN OCEAN

Path of shark Nicole

AUSTRALIA

Particle Collider [Smashing!]

Deep below the French–Swiss border lies the biggest physics experiment ever. The Large Hadron Collider (LHC) is a long, circular tunnel packed with high-tech gear. Here, scientists smash together tiny particles of matter called protons. They hope to see even smaller particles, never observed before.

Magnets accelerate the particles

LHC accelerator tube
Over 9,000 giant magnets help two beams of protons travel faster and faster, and with huge amounts of energy, in opposite directions around the 27-km (17-mile) tunnel. The protons travel at 99.9 per cent the speed of light before crashing into one another.

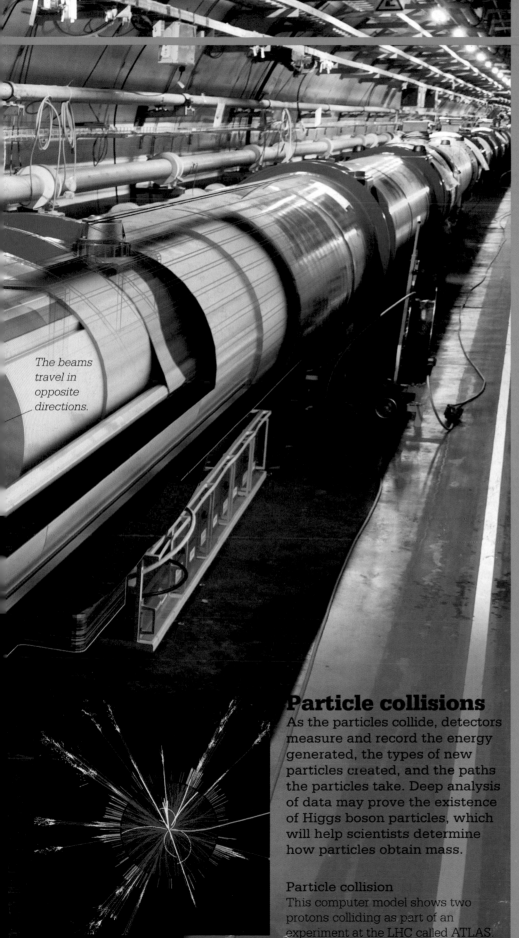

The beams travel in opposite directions.

Seeing the invisible

Human eyes were the most powerful tool for seeing for thousands of years, until the invention of glass lenses. New technologies continue to be developed to help scientists see increasingly smaller and smaller objects.

1021 The first magnifying glasses allowed people to see clearly the body parts of small creatures, such as insects.

CA. 1590 The first optical microscopes were invented. Within a century, new microscopes allowed people to see individual plant cells for the first time.

1931 The first electron microscope, which uses a beam of electrons, was made. Today's scanning electron microscopes (SEMs) can make visible the inner structure of crystals and tiny bacteria.

SEM IMAGE OF AN ANT'S EYE

1981 The scanning tunnelling microscope (STM), a type of electron microscope, was developed. STMs can produce images of individual atoms.

STM IMAGE OF MANGANESE ATOMS

2008 Scientists fired the first protons around the Large Hadron Collider and observed subatomic particles.

Particle collisions

As the particles collide, detectors measure and record the energy generated, the types of new particles created, and the paths the particles take. Deep analysis of data may prove the existence of Higgs boson particles, which will help scientists determine how particles obtain mass.

Particle collision
This computer model shows two protons colliding as part of an experiment at the LHC called ATLAS.

"I think we are on the verge of a revolution in our understanding of the Universe. . . . [The] LHC is certainly, by far, the biggest jump into the unknown."
—BRIAN COX, BRITISH PHYSICIST AT THE LHC

Spies have always used technology in ingenious ways, both to learn an enemy's secrets and to protect their own from discovery. Many of the most famous spy stories date from the Cold War – the period after World War II when the United States and the Soviet Union were great rivals.

BADGE OF THE KGB, THE SOVIET SECRET SERVICE (1954–1991)

Goldfinger (1964)
In this movie, Bond's Aston Martin DB5 car contained machine-guns, a bulletproof screen, and an ejector seat.

Bond . . . James Bond
The most famous fictional spy, James Bond, is always equipped with the latest gear, thanks to technical wizard Q and his team of researchers and engineers. Bond's many gadgets have ranged from tracking devices and a jetpack to an exploding pen.

Spy satellites identify objects the size of an orange from 300 km (185 miles) above Earth's surface

Wheel cipher
In the 1790s, Thomas Jefferson (later the third US president) created a cipher machine. The edge of each of its 26 wheels was randomly marked with the letters of the alphabet. When the wheels were moved to spell out a received sequence of scrambled letters, another row revealed the real message.

Code maker
Jefferson used this machine to turn his documents into code.

THOMAS JEFFERSON (1743–1826)

Listening device
A wooden depiction of the United States' Great Seal hung on a wall in the US embassy in Moscow for over six years. It had been presented as a gift by the Soviet Union in 1945, but in 1952, the embassy discovered that the seal contained a bug. It had been relaying conversations to Soviet spies outside the building.

Eavesdropping
The Soviet spies listened to conversations by bouncing radio waves off the bug.

Sound waves made the bug's cover vibrate, which altered the radio waves returning to the spies.

THE BUGGED GREAT SEAL

Minicamera

MINOX film cameras were used by spies of many nations to copy documents. One such agent was John Walker, a US Navy officer who spied for almost 20 years for the Soviet KGB before his arrest in 1985. He took so many photos that his camera allegedly wore out.

Miniature marvel
Measuring 7.5 cm (3 ins) long and weighing as little as 130 g (4.5 oz), a MINOX camera was small enough to hide in the palm of a spy's hand.

JOHN WALKER, LEFT (B. 1937)

U-2 spy plane

Fast, unarmed spy planes carrying incredibly powerful zoom cameras can fly over enemy territory and monitor what's happening on the ground below. In service since 1955, the Lockheed U-2 plane has flown thousands of spy missions for the USA, and a fleet of 32 U-2s will be in service until at least 2015.

Captured pilot
A U-2 pilot, Gary Powers, was captured by the Soviets in 1960. He was released in a 1962 swap with a US-held KGB spy.

GARY POWERS (1929–77)

Memory stick

Spy tech isn't always about specially made gadgets – spies often use ordinary information technology (IT) devices. In 2010, Russian-born Anna Chapman was arrested in New York. The FBI claimed that she and other spies used USB memory sticks, laptops, and Wi-Fi to exchange secret data.

Hidden in plain sight
Computer data can be stored on a memory stick. No one would suspect that it holds vital secrets.

ANNA CHAPMAN (B. 1982

Online spies

The USA's Cyber Command tries to keep spies from using the Internet to hack into military computer networks to steal data.

Headquarters
Cyber Command operates from this building at the US Army's Fort Meade base in Maryland.

1.8 billion:
the number of attacks on US government computer systems every month

Robots are machines that perform difficult, repetitive, or dangerous tasks for us. Most robots gather information about their surroundings using cameras and other sensors. They then follow instructions given by an onboard computer or sent by remote control.

PackBot specifications

Made by	iRobot, USA
Introduced	2002
Length (minus flippers)	68.6 cm (27 ins)
Width	40.6 cm (16 ins)
Height (arm retracted)	17.8 cm (7 ins)
Weight (minus batteries)	20.4 kg (45 lbs)
Power	2 lithium-ion batteries
Sensors	Accelerometers, compass, GPS, cameras, inclinometer
Top speed	9.3 kph (5.8 mph)

PackBot
A human operator controls this mobile robot from a distance by remote control. PackBot can detect and disarm bombs, handle dangerous chemicals, and even explore damaged nuclear power stations.

PackBot in action
With its surveillance camera, a PackBot peers into a van thought to contain a bomb.

Gripper
This gripper is just one of PackBot's range of arm tools.

Multipurpose roving robot
As PackBot moves, it communicates with its controller. It can carry out a range of tasks using arm tools, called end effectors.

90: the number of seconds it takes to get PackBot up and running

Other PackBot arm tools

FLASHLIGHT | CABLE CUTTER | GLASS BREAKER | ROUTE CLEARANCE TOOL KIT

Tracks and flippers
Mobile robots with legs or with tanklike tracks are better at crossing rough ground than wheeled machines are. PackBot's tracks and movable flippers enable the robot to overcome obstacles in its path.

Rotating flippers

Rounded track belts
Tracks enable PackBot to tackle mud, snow, and steep slopes.

The flippers tilt, and their tracks grip the ground.

Rotating flippers haul the robot over the ridge.

The flippers rotate until they face ahead again.

1 Climbing a ridge
When PackBot reaches the top of a ridge or a sharp dip, the flippers tilt down.

2 Over the top
The flippers then move back and underneath the robot, propelling it forwards.

3 Straight ahead
Having overcome the obstacle, PackBot trundles off at up to 2.6 m (8.5 ft) per second.

bolts]

Surveillance camera
*This colour camera can
magnify up to 312 times.*

LED array
*Bright light-emitting
diode (LED) lamps
illuminate the scene
viewed by the camera.*

Joint sensors
*Sensors in the
joints tell the
controller the
exact position of
the robot's arm.*

Extendable arm
*Able to lift 13.6 kg
(30 lbs), the arm
can also turn and
work around corners.*

Controller
*A microprocessor
in the body
coordinates the
robot's actions.*

Drive camera
*This shows the
route ahead,
and tilts to give
a close view of
the gripper.*

Radio transmitter
*Data and audio signals
are relayed via the
radio transmitter.*

Communications cable
*Cable played out by this spool
links the robot with its operator.*

Robot thinking

Some robots can work on
their own, but they must
still be programmed beforehand
by humans. Massive advances
in programming, computing, and
sensors will be necessary before
robots can be truly intelligent
and able to think for themselves.

Artificial intelligence?
Sci-fi films, such as *I, Robot* (2004),
often feature free-thinking robots, but
that technology is still a long way off.

More here

robotics end effector
sensors **hazmat robots**
mobile robots
robot controllers

*Robot Adventures with
Robosapien™ and Friends:
Introduction to Robotics*
(Vision One Pictures, 2010)

Go to one of the events
held for National Robotics
Week every April (www.
nationalroboticsweek.org).

Visit the robotics collection
at the Massachusetts
Institute of Technology
Museum, Cambridge,
Massachusetts, USA.

accelerometer: a sensor
that detects and measures
movement (see page 47).

autonomous: self-
controlling. Autonomous
robots can work without
human supervision.

inclinometer: a sensor
that can measure the
angles of slopes.

sensor: a device that can
detect (and sometimes
measure) aspects of its
surroundings, such as
heat, light, and movement.

Robosoccer

RoboCup is an annual soccer tournament for robots. It gives robotics students and researchers a chance to test the design, sensors, programming, and autonomy (the ability to make decisions and act without human help) of their machines. Creating successful robot footballers may lead to the development of robots that will be able to work alongside humans.

Robots in action [Tough,

In 1961, the first industrial robot, Unimate 1, began work at a car factory in the USA. Today, millions of robots are in use worldwide. Robots can do work more accurately and for longer than humans, and in conditions too hostile for people to endure.

Canadarm2

This robotic arm moves astronauts, equipment, and cargo around the International Space Station (see pages 82–83). It travels along rails on the outside of the space station.

What does it do?	Works on the ISS
Built by	Canadian Space Agency
Introduced	2001

Fanuc S420i

Able to weld metal parts and also handle heavy loads, the Fanuc S420i has worked in factories for many years. Other industrial robots can spray-paint and handle toxic chemicals.

Welding robot
Sparks fly as a Fanuc S420i welds joints on a car body in an automobile factory.

What does it do?	Welds metal parts together
Built by	Fanuc, Japan
Introduced	1994

Astronaut's assistant
Held by Canadarm2, an astronaut attaches a camera to the ISS.

Da Vinci

Guided by a human surgeon, the Da Vinci robot performs operations in hospitals. It has three arms to wield surgical instruments and one to hold a camera, which relays 3D images back to the surgeon.

DA VINCI ROBOT

What does it do?	Performs surgery under human control
Built by	Intuitive Surgical, Inc., USA
Introduced	1999

More than 8.37 million:
the number of industrial and service robots working worldwide

Autosub3

An autonomous underwater vehicle (AUV), *Autosub3* maps the seabed and does scientific investigations. It can travel for 400 km (250 miles) and dives to a depth of 1,600 m (5,250 ft).

What does it do?	Conducts ocean research
Built by	University of Southampton, UK
Introduced	2005

Polar research
Autosub3 can investigate hard-to-reach places, such as under sea ice.

Gostai Jazz

Robot security guards such as the Gostai Jazz patrol homes, offices, and factories. They raise the alarm when their sensors detect intruders, fire, or smoke.

What does it do?	Guards buildings
Built by	Gostai, France
Introduced	2010

Robot on patrol
The Jazz can follow a programmed route around a building, sending video over the Internet to a human manager.

Digital camera
Using face-recognition software and this digital camera, Autom can identify individual human faces and follow a person's movements.

Eye contact
Electric motors move the eyes to point at a person's face.

Autom
This research robot interacts with people every day to help them change their behaviour, such as eating more healthily. It can talk to encourage them, using speech software linked to an amplifier and speaker.

What does it do?	Acts as a life coach to humans
Built by	MIT Media Lab, USA
Introduced	2007

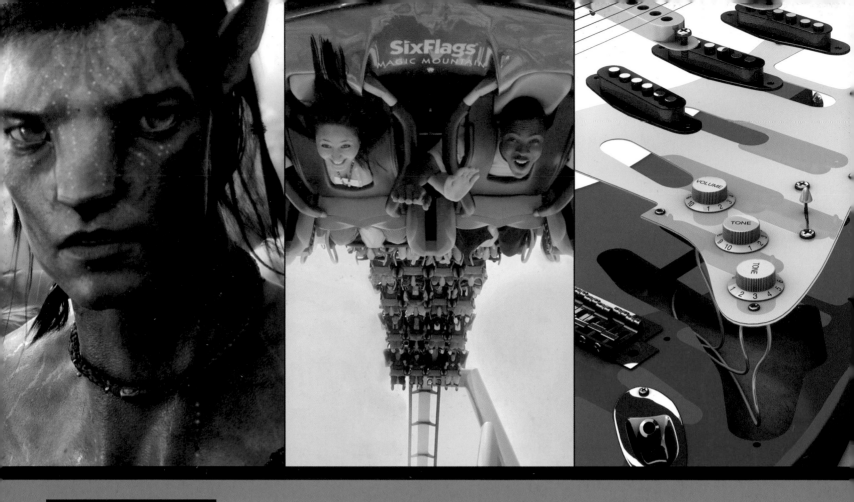

Fun, g
& th

* Why do 3D movies and TV shows seem so real?

* Where are the world's scariest rollercoasters?

* What makes an electric guitar rock?

ames,
rills

Computer gaming [From

The first chess and noughts-and-crosses computer programs were written in the 1950s. But it was the development of microprocessors (see pages 16–17) and personal computers (PCs) in the 1970s that kick-started a gaming revolution.

1977
Atari 2600
This console did not have built-in games. Instead, games had to be loaded from separate cartridges that were plugged into the console.

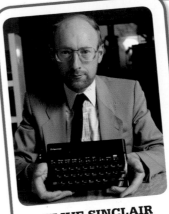

CLIVE SINCLAIR

British inventor

Founded: Sinclair Research Ltd

Developed: ZX80, ZX81, Spectrum, and QL computers

1980–82
Home computing
The introduction of budget computers, including Sinclair computers in the UK and Commodores in North America, led to a boom in home computing. Many video games were developed for these low-cost devices.

1989
Creative Labs' first Sound Blaster card for personal computers brought high-quality sound to PC video games.

1951
British company Ferranti made the Nimrod computer specifically to play the mathematics game Nim.

1967
American Ralph Baer invented the gaming joystick. In 1968, he made a video game console, the Brown Box.

1960•   1970•

Dots represent 10-year increases.

1962
The first action game, Spacewar!, was created by programmers in the USA.

1977
In the USA, Bruce Artwick began work on a flight simulator game – Microsoft's Flight Simulator 1.0 of 1982.

1978
Taito of Japan launched the Space Invaders arcade game, one of the most popular games ever.

1980
Using new graphics techniques, Atari created Battlezone, a three-dimensional (3D) arcade game.

1972
Pong
This arcade tennis game from US company Atari was the first commercially successful video game. A version for use on home TVs came out in 1975.

PLAYING PONG ON A TV SET, 1977

SHIGERU MIYAMOTO

Japanese designer

Company: Nintendo

Developed: Donkey Kong, Mario, Legend of Zelda

1981
Donkey Kong
Designed by Shigeru Miyamoto, Nintendo's Donkey Kong was one of the first "platform" games. These games require the player to overcome obstacles and jump between suspended platforms.

SCENE FROM DONKEY KONG

Pong to Wii]

1998
Dance Dance Revolution

The first commercially successful arcade dancing game, Dance Dance Revolution, was produced by Konami. A version with a plastic dance mat for home gaming consoles went on sale soon after.

ARCADE VERSION OF DANCE DANCE REVOLUTION

75.66 million:
the number of copies of Wii Sports sold by 2011, making it the bestselling computer game ever

2006
Nintendo Wii

This system uses a handheld wireless controller, the Wii Remote, to sense the movements of the gamer (see page 47).

WII CONTROLLER AND CONSOLE

1994

The Hagenuk MT-2000 was the first mobile phone with a built-in game, the falling brick puzzle game Tetris.

2006

The newly released Sony PlayStation 3 (PS3) and Nintendo Wii consoles battled with the Microsoft Xbox 360 (2005) for popularity.

•1990 •2000 2010

2000

Electronic Arts published The Sims, which simulated the daily lives of people in a suburban house.

2004

Nintendo released its DS handheld game system, the first with a touch screen and a microphone.

2010

Sony released the PlayStation Move motion-sensing controller for the PS3 console.

2010
Xbox Kinect

Kinect, for Microsoft's Xbox 360, detects motion without the use of a handheld controller (see page 47).

KICKING ACTION WITH KINECT

WAVEBIRD CONTROLLER

2002
Going wireless

The first wireless controller, the WaveBird, was released for Nintendo's GameCube. It sent signals to the console via radio waves.

2005
Guitar Hero

First produced for Sony's PlayStation 2 console, this music game has a guitar-shaped controller.

GUITAR HERO CONTROLLER

Gam s controll r [Sensing

For video games to work well, players need fast, responsive controllers to send commands back to the console. Many devices now use motion sensing, in which the whole controller is moved to simulate actions in a game, from thrusting a sword to hitting a ball.

Mobile gaming

Many games on smartphones or tablets use the device's touch screen to provide game controls. Others, such as racing games, use accelerometers (see next page) to make cars or characters move.

Angry Birds
Run on operating systems (see page 20) such as Apple iOS, Android, and Symbian, Angry Birds uses touchscreen controls to catapult birds around the screen.

500 million copies of Rovio's Angry Birds game have been sold since its 2009 release

Joystick

Early joysticks, like the Atari 2600 stick, were gripped with the whole hand. Many modern joysticks are smaller, built into gamepads, and controlled by a player's thumb.

ATARI 2600 JOYSTICK, 1977

PAC-MAN

Switches
Pushing a joystick in one direction closes a switch on its base. This sends a signal indicating whether the joystick was pushed left, right, forwards, or backwards.

Forward movement

Joystick

Circuit
Pressing the contact completes the circuit.

Sensor
This sends a signal to the console.

Contact switch

Contact switch

Force feedback

Found in joysticks and gamepads, this feature makes the controller wobble or vibrate, giving a sensation of force when a car crashes or a character hits a wall during a game.

NINTENDO 64 CONTROLLER, 1996

DIDDY KONG RACING

Turning axle

Electric motor

Offset cam
This off-centre weight creates vibrations inside the controller.

Electric motor housing

Rumble pack
This pack plugs into a controller. It has a motor that spins an off-centre weight and causes the controller to vibrate when the game action gets exciting.

motion]

Motion sensing

Accelerometers (see below) sense changes in the controller's speed and direction of movement, which are converted into on-screen actions.

WII REMOTE, NINTENDO, 2006

Body motion sensing

Microsoft's Kinect does not need a physical controller. The player's motions are scanned and tracked by sensors. The console translates this movement into actions within the game.

3D depth sensor

Colour camera

3D depth sensor

KINECT FOR XBOX 360, MICROSOFT, 2010

iCONTROLPAD GAMEPAD, 2011

Mobile controllers

Add-on Bluetooth devices provide gaming controls for smartphones and tablets. The iControlPad unit has direction, movement, option, and fire buttons.

WII SPORTS BASEBALL

DANCE CENTRAL

VELOCISPIDER

Capacitive accelerometer

Direction of movement

Sensor
This calculates speed and movement from changes in the charge.

Charge plate

Silicon bar
As it moves, the bar changes the amount of electrical charge.

Charge plate

Movement bends a silicon bar, altering the charge between two plates. A sensor then calculates the controller's acceleration.

---

3 Displaying
The player's movements are converted into actions in the game.

1 Sensing
The Kinect IR sensor recognizes a player standing in its depth picture.

2 Tracking
The sensor tracks moving body parts, up to 30 times each second.

Infrared (IR)

A projector sends out IR light, which bounces back to the console. A camera collects the light and builds an image of the room and the player's position.

Smartphone
The phone's Bluetooth chip receives the signals and sends data back to the controller.

Radio signals

Controller
A Bluetooth chip inside sends signals carrying the player's instructions.

Bluetooth

This low-power radio technology allows a games controller and a smartphone, console, or tablet to communicate over distances of up to 10 m (33 feet).

Camcorder [Capturing the

Digital cameras use microchip technology (see pages 15–17) to record images. Still cameras capture a single image, or frame, but camcorders record multiple images one after another, often at a rate of 25 or 30 frames per second. Replayed at the same rate, the individual frames seem to merge to produce a moving picture.

Digital signal processor (DSP)
The DSP uses electrical signals from the CCD to build up pictures that it sends on to the memory controller and the viewfinder.

Film reels
Until the 1990s, most movies were shot on reels of film coated with chemicals that reacted when exposed to light. The film was developed (processed chemically in darkness) before the movie could be projected onto a screen.

Hard disk
Some camcorders have small hard disks that can store many gigabytes of videos and images.

How a digital camcorder works

Inside a camcorder, lenses focus light from a scene onto a sensor chip, called a charge-coupled device (CCD), which converts light into electrical signals. These are processed into data to form digital images. A camcorder can make over 1,000 images every minute.

Memory controller
The flow of digital data into and out of the camcorder's memory is controlled by this microprocessor.

Lens housing
This unit contains a set of lenses, the electric motors of the zoom mechanism, and the autofocus.

Ultraviolet (UV) filter
Made of glass or plastic, this filter cuts out some of the glare caused by UV rays from the Sun.

Lens fittings
Filters can be screwed into the lens barrel to improve or alter the scene – for example, by giving it an old-fashioned sepia colour.

Light
A small lamp can brighten the scene being recorded.

Rechargeable battery
The lithium-ion battery (see page 21) can provide power for up to ten hours of video recording.

Viewfinder
A sample of the image captured by the lens and the CCD is sent to the viewfinder, showing the user how the video will look.

Viewfinder lens unit

Playback controls
These controls allow the user to pause, fast-forward, rewind, and zoom in and out.

Memory card
A small digital memory card is used to transfer videos to a computer.

CCD chip
Thousands of tiny components on this microchip convert light into electrical signals, which are sent to the DSP.

Input and output ports
Cables attach to these sockets so that the camcorder can play its movies on a television or computer.

Microphone
Sounds are converted into digital audio signals that form the sound track to the video.

Fold-out display
The touchscreen menu on this display is used to select recording options. Recorded videos can also be viewed on the display.

Liquid crystal display (LCD)

Back-light unit

Circuit board

Camera autofocus

An autofocus mechanism judges how far away an object is and adjusts the lens so the image is sharp. Some do this with mini-lenses and sensors that detect the distance between light rays coming from the edges of the main lens.

Focus point   Lens   Mini-lens   Sensor
FOCUSSED
Beam splitter

Focussed
If the image is properly focussed, light rays strike sensors the correct distance apart.

FOCUS TOO NEAR

Focus too near
If the lens is focussed too near, the light rays strike the sensors too close together.

FOCUS TOO FAR

Focus too far
If the lens is focussed too far, the light rays strike the sensors too far apart.

3D [In the picture]

When you watch something in 3D, this optical technology tricks your brain into viewing images the same way as you see everyday life. Movie, TV, and games creators use special digital cameras and screens to create 3D effects. With 3D glasses, the illusion of depth puts you in the middle of the action.

Natural 3D

Your eyes view scenes in two dimensions (2D). To see the world in 3D – with objects appearing at different distances – your brain processes the image that each eye sees and uses the slight differences between them to build a 3D scene.

Combined 3D view

LEFT VIEW   RIGHT VIEW

Optic nerves connect to the brain.

Stereopsis
Each eye sees the same scene from a slightly different angle. Your brain puts the two views together to create a 3D image. This process is known as stereopsis.

3D technology

A 3D movie or TV show is filmed with several cameras that capture slightly different views of the same scene. A special viewing device, screen, or pair of glasses then directs each of the separate images to a different eye.

Two photos

One hole for each eye

Stereoscope
This early 3D device uses two 2D images of a scene taken from slightly different viewpoints. Each eye views one image through the stereoscope. The brain merges the two images into a single 3D picture.

Red projector

Blue projector

This filter blocks blue.   This filter blocks red.

Red and blue
Many 3D TV and cinema systems project two views of the scene in different colours. 3D glasses have a different coloured filter in each lens. The filters only let certain colours through to each eye.

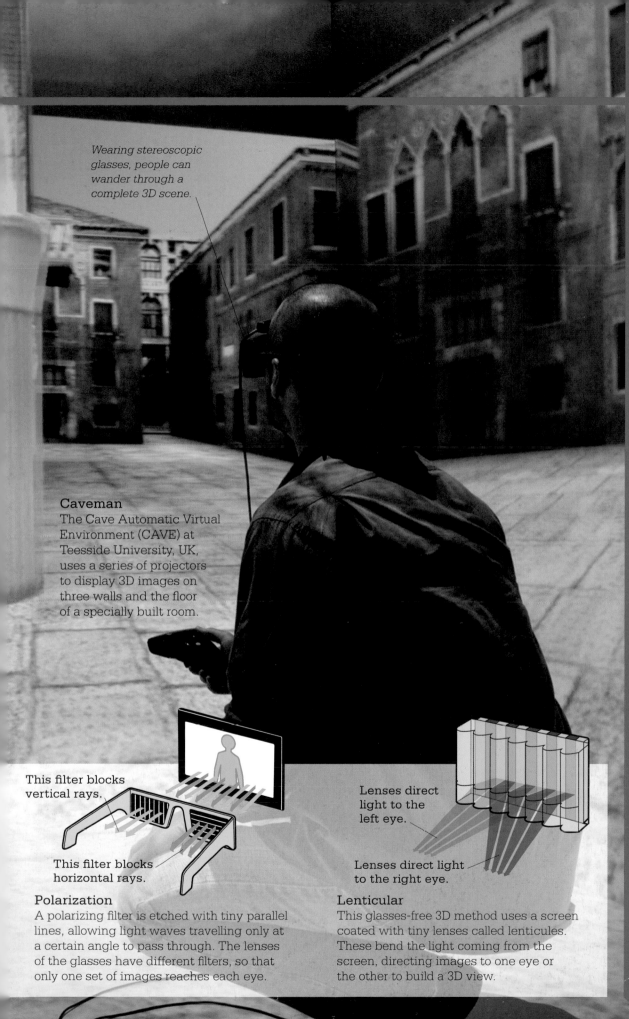

Wearing stereoscopic glasses, people can wander through a complete 3D scene.

Caveman
The Cave Automatic Virtual Environment (CAVE) at Teesside University, UK, uses a series of projectors to display 3D images on three walls and the floor of a specially built room.

This filter blocks vertical rays.

This filter blocks horizontal rays.

Polarization
A polarizing filter is etched with tiny parallel lines, allowing light waves travelling only at a certain angle to pass through. The lenses of the glasses have different filters, so that only one set of images reaches each eye.

Lenses direct light to the left eye.

Lenses direct light to the right eye.

Lenticular
This glasses-free 3D method uses a screen coated with tiny lenses called lenticules. These bend the light coming from the screen, directing images to one eye or the other to build a 3D view.

More here

CAVE 3D TV stereoscope **polarized 3D glasses** stereopsis lenticular TV screen

Search the web for the nearest IMAX cinema, where exciting 3D films are shown on huge screens.

The 3D Centre of Art and Photography in Portland, Oregon, USA, is the world's first art gallery and museum dedicated to 3D images.

NINTENDO 3DS FACT FILE

Introduced: February 2011

3D screen: 9 cm (3.5 in)

Size: 13.4 cm x 7.3 cm x 2 cm (5.3 in x 2.9 in x 0.8 in)

Weight: 226 g (8 oz)

Worldwide sales: 6.7 million (as of October 2011)

lenticular lens: a curved lens that allows each eye to see a different image of the same object at exactly the same time.

stereoscopic 3D: a system that uses two images, one for each eye, to create a 3D effect.

Milestones in 3D

For more than a century, inventors have tried to create realistic movies in three dimensions (3D). Recent advances may soon make glasses-free 3D viewing the norm, both at home and at the movies.

1894 British film pioneer William Friese-Greene patented a 3D movie process, using a stereoscope (see page 50) to view two films shown side by side.

1922 *The Power of Love* was the first 3D film shown to a paying audience.

1952 *Bwana Devil*, an adventure film, was the first 3D movie in colour.

1986 IMAX cinemas showed the first 3D documentaries on huge screens.

2009 A new kind of 3D camera was used for the movie *Avatar* to give more depth to the 3D scenes.

SCENE FROM *AVATAR* (2009)

JAN. 2010 Panasonic introduced the largest 3D TV so far, with a screen measuring 386 centimetres (152 ins) diagonally.

LENTICULAR SCREEN OF 3D TV

OCT. 2010 Toshiba released the first glasses-free 3D TV, which used a lenticular screen (see page 51).

"With 3D projection . . . audiences will be seeing something that was never technically possible before!"
—JAMES CAMERON, DIRECTOR OF *AVATAR*

Sounds amazing

Sounds are waves of energy that travel away from the sound's source. From the 19th century onwards, new technologies have provided different ways to capture and record sounds so that they can be stored and replayed later.

Travelling sound

Sound waves travel as vibrations through a medium, such as air. Sounds vary in pitch (whether the tone is high or low) and in amplitude (the amount of energy the waves have). The greater the amplitude, the louder the sound will be when it reaches your ears.

HIGH-FREQUENCY WAVE

AMPLITUDE

TIME

LOW-FREQUENCY WAVE

Peak

Trough

Wavelength is the distance between troughs or peaks.

High or low? Frequency is the number of waves per second. A greater frequency produces sound of a higher pitch.

Gramophone
Invented in the 1890s, the gramophone replayed sounds held on flat discs. Called records, these discs stored analogue sounds as tiny bumps and dips cut into a spiral groove on the disc.

MP3 files

The MP3 format is a way of storing digital sound files so that they take up less memory space. Software in a computer or MP3 player, such as an iPod, analyzes a track's sound waves and removes parts that are not needed.

AUDIO CD

Sound selection
Sounds that the human ear cannot hear are deleted by compression.

Storing more

Early gramophone records often had one track, or song, on each side of the disc. Here are the typical numbers of tracks on later storage formats.

14
Vinyl album *Long-playing (LP) records hold 52 minutes of sound.*

25
C90 cassette *A reel of magnetic tape inside stores 1.5 hours of audio.*

[It's playback time!]

940% increase

2004   2009

Download

Digital downloads
The market for digital music downloads boomed between 2004 and 2009. Legal downloaded digital music sales worldwide in 2010 totalled more than $4.6 billion.

Each color is a different sound wave in a song.

Loud sound
A loud sound wave masks other sounds at a particular point in a sound file.

Space saver
Sounds masked by a loud sound are not included in the MP3 file.

Loudness
The decibel scale is a measure of the intensity, or loudness, of a sound. A sound that is 10 decibels greater than another sound is 10 times louder. So a 20-decibel increase is 100 times louder (10 x 10), and a 30-decibel increase is 1,000 times louder (10 x 10 x 10).

Near and far
Here are some typical sounds and their ratings on the decibel scale when heard from nearby. Sounds lose energy and loudness the further they have to travel.

How compression works
Compression removes very high- or low-pitched sounds beyond the range of human hearing, and also those masked, or covered, by louder sounds. The resulting MP3 file may be 90 per cent smaller than the original.

MP3 PLAYER

iPod
Sounds are stored as digital data files in an iPod's memory. When replayed, a sound processor and digital-to-analogue converter chips turn the digital data back into sound waves.

JET ENGINE 140 DECIBELS

JACKHAMMER 120 DECIBELS

CAR HORN 110 DECIBELS

CHAINSAW 100 DECIBELS

TRAIN 80 DECIBELS

HAIR DRYER 90 DECIBELS

WHISPER 40 DECIBELS

WIND TURBINE 50 DECIBELS

312 million iPods were sold by mid-2011

iPod   MENU

22
CD *One-sided compact discs hold up to 80 minutes of sound.*

1,000
DVD *A digital versatile disc can store up to 4.7 gigabytes of data.*

40,000
160GB MP3 player
This can play a new song every day for 109 years.

In the 1930s, the invention of the electric guitar changed music forever. This new technology ushered in rock, indie, punk, metal, and many more styles besides. Played unplugged, an electric guitar is very quiet. Its vibrating strings need electrical amplification to really rock!

Strings
Each string is of a different thickness, so each produces different notes.

Pickup covers

Pickups
A pickup detects the vibrations of the strings (see opposite page). Below each string is a permanent magnet. The six magnets are wrapped in a coil of copper wire.

Pickguard
Usually made of plastic, this thin sheet protects the guitar's body from scratches.

Fender Stratocaster
Green Day lead guitarist Billie Joe Armstrong plays a Fender Stratocaster. First made in 1954, the "Strat" has been played by many great guitarists, including Jimi Hendrix and U2's The Edge.

Volume control
Turning this knob increases or decreases the volume.

VOLUME
10 1 2 3

TONE
8 9 10 1 2 3

TONE
1 2 3 4 5 6

Anatomy of a guitar
Like other electric guitars, the Fender Stratocaster has six strings made of metal wire. They are held taut between the bridge and the tuning pegs. The harder a string is struck, the more it vibrates – and the louder the sound it makes when plugged into an amplifier.

Metal bridge
The strings attach here, supported by six small grooves called saddles.

Jack socket
This is where you plug in the jack lead – the cable that connects the guitar to an amplifier.

Strap hook
The guitar's shoulder strap fixes onto this hook.

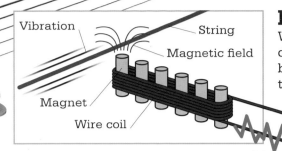

Vibration
String
Magnetic field
Magnet
Wire coil

How pickups work

When a guitar string is played, its vibration disturbs the force field produced by the magnet beneath it. This causes an electric current to flow through the wire coil.

Tuning pegs
These geared pegs can be turned to alter the strings' pitch.

Signal from pickup
A signal in the form of a varying electric current is sent through the guitar's wiring to the jack socket.

Electrical signal

Headstock
The wooden head holds the tuning pegs.

1,220 m
(4,000 ft): the length of the copper wire in the coil of a typical guitar pickup

Fretboard
Pressing the fingers down here changes the length of each string and its pitch.

Pickup selector
This switch determines which pickups are used. Each pickup gives a distinctive sound.

Pump up the volume

The signal from an electric guitar needs to be boosted in power. An amplifier receives the signal, increases its strength, and sends it to a loudspeaker. The loudspeaker converts the signal back into sounds, which are louder than those originally made by the strings.

Tone controls
Turning up the knobs gives a "brighter" sound with more treble.

Strengthened signal from amplifier

AMPLIFIER

SIGNAL FROM GUITAR

Weak signal from guitar

Loudspeaker
Sound waves travel out from the loudspeaker as vibrations in the air.

Cone
The moving coil causes the cone to vibrate, generating sound waves.

Wooden body
With a body made of wood such as alder, maple, or ash, an electric guitar typically weighs 3–5 kg (6.5–11 lbs).

Signal in
The electrical signal enters the metal coil.

Metal coil
The coil becomes an electromagnet, creating a changing magnetic field.

Movement
The permanent magnet and the electromagnet attract and repel each other, making the coil move to and fro.

Control cavity
Parts of the body are hollowed out to hold the wiring from the guitar's pickups and the controls to the jack socket.

Permanent magnet

Go to any theme park and you'll find that the longest queues are for the rollercoasters. These rides are closed circuits of twisting, dipping tracks on which cars carrying thrill-seekers whizz by at high speeds. Strap yourself in and check out this nerve-shredding selection of coasters.

Strata

Rollercoasters with drops along their length totalling over 120 m (400 ft) are called strata coasters. Only two have been built so far, the taller of which is Kingda Ka (below).

Name	Kingda Ka, Six Flags Great Adventure, USA
Cool fact	Highest point is 139 m (456 ft)
Introduced	2005

Launch

Powerful electric motors or hydraulic (pressurized-liquid) systems can launch riders to superfast speeds almost instantly. Dodonpa (left), in Japan, uses another launch method – compressed air – to send riders racing down its 1,189 m (3,901 ft) track.

Name	Dodonpa, Fuji-Q Highland, Japan
Cool fact	0–172 kph (0–107 mph) in 1.8 seconds
Introduced	2001

Hair-raising high-rise
Dodonpa's carriages are propelled over a vertical part of the track that is as high as a 17-storey building.

Dizzying drop
This picture shows the view from the "top hat" hill of Kingda Ka, featuring a fearsome drop longer than a football field.

Cable lift

Many rides, including El Toro (below), start with a slow rise to the highest part of the track, with the cars hauled up by a winch or cable system. Then they plummet down a steep slope, powered by gravity.

Name	El Toro, Six Flags Great Adventure, USA
Cool fact	Wooden, with a 76-degree slope
Introduced	2006

Fastest

Formula Rossa, in Abu Dhabi's Ferrari World theme park, is the fastest rollercoaster in the world. Riders wear protective glasses as their cars roar from 0 to 100 kph (0 to 62 mph) in just 2 seconds.

FORMULA ROSSA

240 kph (150 mph): the maximum speed **Formula Rossa reaches along its** 2.1 km (1.3-mile) course

Flying

Suspended in a horizontal position like flying superheroes, the riders are flung around swooping turns and soaring lifts in the tracks.

Name	Flying Coaster, Genting, Malaysia
Cool fact	Riders experience 3.6 times the force of gravity
Introduced	2004

Terrifying Toro
As the carriages hurtle down the slope, they build up enough speed to carry them around the rest of the ride.

Extreme force
On flying coasters, speeds are usually slower than 96 kph (60 mph), but thrills are high due to the unusual angle of the cars.

Inversion

On this type of ride, the passengers are suspended beneath the track on chairs or in pods. The chairs invert (flip upside-down) on corkscrewing bends and turns, disorienting the riders. The UK's Nemesis (above) was the first inversion rollercoaster in Europe.

Name	Nemesis, Alton Towers, UK
Cool fact	The ride includes 4 inversions
Introduced	1994

Midair inversion
Nemesis passengers are flipped over in midair during their thrilling 716-m (2,349-ft) ride, which also passes through an underground tunnel.

Theme-park thrills

Riders hurtle along at up to 100 kph (62 mph) on the Tatsu rollercoaster at Six Flags Magic Mountain in California. Designed and modelled with computers, cutting-edge rides use sudden acceleration and changes in angle to give serious thrills. Passengers are launched at high speed, flipped upside down, and hurled around the track's corkscrewing twists.

Force, s

pov

* Do jet skis use jet engines?

* How does a space rocket overcome Earth's gravity?

* Which car smashed the sound barrier?

peed, &

wer

Engines and motors

Flick a switch, turn a key, or push a button, and machines burst into life. It's all thanks to engines and motors – devices that convert fuel or electrical energy into force and movement.

Internal combustion engine

Most cars are powered by internal combustion engines. A mixture of fuel and air is burned in the engine's cylinders, forcing pistons up and down. A crankshaft changes this motion into a turning movement that drives the car's wheels.

1,360 kg (3,000 lb) of air is drawn into a GE90 jet engine every second

The inlet valve opens, letting in fuel and air.

The piston moves down.

The crankshaft turns.

The inlet valve shuts.

The rising piston squeezes the mixture.

The spark plug provides a spark to ignite the mixture.

Gases push the piston down.

The exhaust valve opens.

Waste gases escape.

The piston drives the gases up.

1 Intake
Air and fuel are drawn into an engine cylinder as a piston moves down.

2 Compression
The piston then rises to compress (squeeze) the air and fuel mixture.

3 Ignition
The mixture is lit. As it burns, the expanding gases force the piston back down.

4 Exhaust
The piston rises again, forcing the waste gases out of the cylinder.

[The power providers]

Electric motor

Inside a motor is a wire coil surrounded by the force field of a magnet. When electricity flows through the coil, the coil produces its own magnetic field. The two fields push and pull on each other, making the coil rotate. This motion is used to power machinery.

Commutator
This changes the current's direction every half turn.

Current
Electricity from a battery or generator flows around the coil.

Magnet

Magnetic force field

Coil

The magnet's poles attract and repel the coil.

How the coil turns
Magnetic attraction pulls the coil up on one side. When the commutator changes the direction of the current, the forces on the coil reverse. The coil is repelled, and pushed down on the other side.

Jet engine

The thrust (force) that pushes a jet aircraft forwards is created by a stream of hot, high-speed, rapidly expanding gases that shoot out from the rear of the engine.

Air intake
Cold air is drawn in at the front of the engine.

Combustion chamber
The air is mixed with fuel and ignited in the combustion chamber.

Parts of a jet engine
Fuel is burned in the combustion chamber. The compressor and turbine are linked by a shaft.

Rotating crankshaft

Compressor
A series of spinning fans compresses the air and forces it backwards.

Turbine
Turned by expanding waste gases as they escape, this set of bladed wheels drives the compressor.

Exhaust nozzle
Waste gases zoom out of the nozzle much faster than air enters the engine.

World's biggest jet engine
Each mighty GE90-115B engine on this Boeing 777-300ER airliner is able to produce up to 58,000 kg (127,900 lbs) of thrust.

Supercar [Fast and furious]

The Bugatti Veyron is one of the world's most desirable supercars. These high-tech sports cars offer the ultimate in performance and style, but at a high price. The Veyron, which holds the road car records for speed and acceleration, can cost up to $2.4 million.

Veyron 16.4 specifications	
Made by	Bugatti, France
Introduced	2005
Engine 16 cylinders; 1,050 horsepower	
0–100 kph (0–62 mph)	2.5 seconds
0–200 kph (0–124 mph)	7.3 seconds
0–300 kph (0–186 mph)	16.7 seconds
Top speed	431 kph (267 mph)
Braking: 400–0 kph (248–0 mph)	Less than 10 seconds

Streamlined car
The curved shape lets air pass smoothly over the car.

BUGATTI BRESCIA, 1925

Racing heritage
Founded in 1909 in France, Bugatti has a long history of making ultrafast cars with powerful engines. In the 1920s and 1930s, Bugatti cars won more than 2,000 races.

Car body
The strong yet lightweight carbon-fibre body is about 4.5 m (14.5 ft) long and 1.2 m (4 ft) high.

Seats
The leather-covered seats contain heaters to warm them up on cold days.

Powerful performer

The Veyron is built by hand in Alsace, France. Its engine produces up to eight times the power of a typical sedan car. The suspension, engine, and other systems (including the air pressure in each tyre) are computer-controlled, ensuring that the car always gives peak performance.

Turbochargers
Four turbochargers boost the engine's power.

Tyres
Special "run-flat" tyres can be driven on even if punctured.

Gearshift
The driver changes gears using small paddlelike switches on the steering wheel.

Wheels
The 50-cm (20-in) wheels are made of a metal mixture called an alloy.

Gearbox
This contains seven gears, each of which changes the speed of the driveshaft and the amount of force it turns with.

Driveshaft
This transfers power from the engine to all four wheels.

Spoiler
The spoiler acts as a brake at high speeds, and it also produces a downward force to help keep the car on the road.

Air ducts
Openings in the roof let air flow into the rear of the car to help cool the brakes and the engine.

Crash protection
Some Veyrons have side-impact bars in the doors to protect the driver and passengers in a broadside collision.

Fuel tank
Made of 250 parts, the tank holds about 100 litres (22 gallons) of fuel.

Engine pistons
The 16 pistons are arranged in 4 angled rows. Each moves up and down inside its own cylinder.

Speed on the road
The sleek lines of a Bugatti Veyron help it travel at top speed. Above 200 kph (137 mph), the body automatically lowers over the wheels to help grip the road.

2.3 seconds:
how long it takes for a Veyron to brake from 100 kph (62 mph) to a complete standstill

Compact engine
The Veyron's compact but powerful internal combustion engine (see page 64) burns fuel in 16 cylinders.

Heat-resistant brakes
The brake discs must withstand the extreme heat produced by friction when braking at high speed.

Power booster
A turbocharger squashes the air entering an engine so that more is forced into the cylinders. This enables extra fuel to be burned, increasing the power output.

Compressor

Linking shaft

Turbine

Air is drawn into the turbocharger.

Exhaust gases from burning fuel in the cylinder are released.

Compressed air

Piston

Engine cylinder

A cooler ensures that the air is at the right temperature.

How it works
The engine's exhaust gases turn a set of blades called a turbine. The rotating turbine spins a wheel called a compressor. This draws in air and compresses (squashes) it before the air enters the cylinders.

Cars [Technology in motion]

Developed in the late 19th century, the earliest automobiles were slow, unreliable, and difficult to control, but they heralded a transport revolution. Today, over 500 million motor vehicles carry people and goods in every country around the globe.

1938
The "people's car"
In Germany, work began on the Volkswagen ("people's car"). Nicknamed the Beetle, this simple, affordable car was made in huge numbers – over 21 million were built between 1938 and 2003.

1885
Petrol-powered car
German engineer Karl Benz's Motorwagen was the first car with an internal combustion engine (see page 64). The engine burned petrol and air to generate power.

BENZ MOTORWAGEN

VOLKSWAGEN BEETLE

1769
In France, Nicolas Cugnot built a three-wheeled, steam-powered wagon that moved at walking speed.

1912
US policeman Lester Wire invented the first electric traffic lights, with red for stop and green for go.

1934
In the UK, "cat's eye" road studs were patented. Cat's eyes reflect the light from headlamps to show drivers the way ahead on dark roads.

•1770   •1900   •1920   •1950

Dots represent 10-year increases.

1891
France's Michelin brothers patented a pneumatic (air-filled) tyre that, when punctured, could be taken off the wheel and repaired.

1912
Electric ignition was invented in the USA by Charles Kettering, allowing cars to be started without turning a crank handle.

1963
The Swedish manufacturer Volvo became the first to equip its cars with seat belts.

1949
Sierra Sam
Sam was the first crash-test dummy – a life-size doll with sensors to test how an accident impacts on the body. The tests are used to make cars safer.

CRASH-TEST DUMMIES

1908
Ford Model T
Henry Ford's Model T was the first car to be mass-produced on a moving assembly line in a factory. The cheap, reliable Model T led to a boom in car ownership.

FORD MODEL T ASSEMBLY LINE, MICHIGAN, USA, 1913

32
kph (20 mph):
the maximum speed limit imposed in the UK by the 1903 Motor Car Act

1979
First monster truck

The monster truck Bigfoot went on show in the USA for the first time. Monster trucks, such as Samson (above), have giant wheels and powerful suspensions. They can climb over large obstacles such as old cars in races and shows.

1987
Ferrari F40

The F40 was the first road car to reach a speed of 322 kph (200 mph). It was created to commemorate the 40th anniversary of the founding of the Ferrari car company by Enzo Ferrari, a former racing driver.

ENZO FERRARI
Italian manufacturer

Founded:	Ferrari S.p.A.
Developed:	Fast, stylish cars

1981
Mercedes-Benz S-Class cars were fitted with an airbag that inflated to protect the driver in a crash.

2005
The Bugatti Veyron, the world's fastest sports car, was launched. Top speed: 407 kph (253 mph).

Dots represent 5-year increases.

•**1975**   •**1990**   •**2000**

1972
The anti-lock braking system (ABS) was invented by Bosch in Germany. It keeps brakes from locking and causing skidding.

1974
Catalytic converters were introduced in the USA. A "cat" removes some of the toxins from exhaust gases.

1997
The launch takes place of the Toyota Prius – a "hybrid" car with both a petrol engine and an electric motor.

1998
The Smart Car was first sold in Europe. With a small engine and only two seats, it is designed for short trips in towns and cities.

1988
Head-up display

The Oldsmobile Cutlass Supreme was the first car with a head-up display (HUD). HUDs beam an image of the dash instruments onto the windscreen, so the driver doesn't have to look down.

HEAD-UP DISPLAY ON A SPORTS CAR

48:
the number of lithium–ion batteries that power the Nissan LEAF to its top speed of 145 kph (90 mph)

2010
Electric family car

The Nissan LEAF electric car went on sale in Japan and the USA. It can travel 100 kilometres (60 miles) on one charge, and produces no waste gas emissions.

NISSAN LEAF

Extreme speed [Smashing

Meet the vehicles for which extreme speed is routine. The fastest vehicles in their class, they are the results of many years of development and testing. Constant improvements to their power and aerodynamics have turned them into machines that can slice through the air at maximum velocity.

Sikorsky X2

Hovering is easy for helicopters, but few fly faster than 322 kph (200 mph). In 2010, aided by an extra push from its rear propeller, the Sikorsky X2 set a new record of 481 kph (299 mph).

What it is	Fastest helicopter
Built by	Sikorsky, USA
Introduced	2008

SR-71 Blackbird

Designed to fly high and fast to spy on enemies below, the SR-71 is the fastest jet aircraft ever made. In 1976, one zoomed to a top speed of 3,530 kph (2,193 mph). It was retired from service in 1998.

What it is	Fastest jet aircraft
Built by	Lockheed, USA
Introduced	1966

High-flying Blackbird
An SR-71 soars high over the Sierra Nevada mountains, California. The jet could climb to 24,390 m (80,258 ft).

Twinset
The X2 research helicopter has two sets of rotors, one above the other.

Suzuki Hayabusa

The Hayabusa's engine is as big as that of a hatchback car, but it is engineered to produce much more power. This superbike has reached speeds of up to 312 kph (194 mph).

What it is	Fastest road motorcycle
Built by	Suzuki, Japan
Introduced	1999

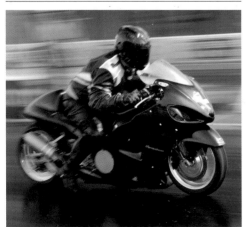

Awesome acceleration
The Hayabusa can go from 0 to 96 kph (0 to 60 mph) in less than 3 seconds.

Rocket sled

In 1954, John Stapp of the US Air Force became the fastest man on Earth. The rocket sled he was strapped to propelled him along at 1,017 kph (632 mph). That's faster than a bullet shot from a revolver!

Sonic Wind No. 1
Stapp's sled, called Sonic Wind No.1, travelled along rails. The sled was used to research human safety at high speeds.

CRH380A

Racing along specially built tracks at 355 kph (221 mph), China's CRH380A electric trains link the cities of Shanghai, Nanjing, and Hangzhou. On a test run in 2010, a CRH380A hit 486 kph (302 mph) – a record for a wheeled rail vehicle (John Stapp's rocket sled went faster – see above).

What it is	Fastest wheeled rail vehicle
Built by	CSR, China
Introduced	2010

Long haul
China's CRH380A locomotive pulls eight carriages, each with up to 85 passengers.

Big burners
Mounted on either side of the driver's cockpit, ThrustSSC's immense jet engines burned around 18 litres (4.8 gallons) of fuel every second!

1,241 kph (771 mph):
the top speed achieved by ThrustSSC in 1997, in the Black Rock Desert, Nevada

ThrustSSC
Powered by two jet engines (see page 65) normally used in Phantom military planes, ThrustSSC set a new world land speed record in 1997. Over two runs, it averaged 1,229 kph (763 mph).

What it is	Fastest land vehicle
Built by	ThrustSSC Project, UK
Introduced	1996

Breaking the sound barrier
ThrustSSC was the first "car" to go faster than sound. Here, it creates a shock wave as it breaks the sound barrier in the Nevada desert.

Racing powerboat

A Formula 1 powerboat momentarily takes to the air off the coast of Kiev, Ukraine. A 425-horsepower engine thrusts the boat's lightweight carbon-fibre hull over the water's surface with great force. Powerboats are phenomenally fast. They can accelerate from a standstill to 160 kph (100 mph) in 4 seconds and can reach a top speed of just over 225 kph (130 mph).

Takeoff [Getting airborne]

Planes and helicopters are heavy. The heaviest of all, the Antonov An-225 cargo plane, has a maximum takeoff weight of 580 tonnes. So how do aircraft get off the ground and into the air? The answer is a force called lift.

274 kg

(605 lbs): the weight of the world's first aircraft, the Wright *Flyer*

Aeroplanes

To set off down the runway, an aeroplane's engine must produce enough thrust to overcome a force called drag, which resists forward movement. As the plane increases in speed, the flow of air around its wings generates an upward force called lift. When lift exceeds the weight of the plane, the aircraft rises into the air.

LIFT

DRAG

THRUST

WEIGHT

Forces on an aircraft
To take off, thrust must be greater than drag, and lift must exceed weight. Once airborne, the aircraft flies level if the forces remain equal.

Airbus A380
This 853-seat airliner, the world's largest plane, has four jet engines. Its 80-m (260-ft) wingspan gives a huge amount of lift.

Aerofoils

Wings are aerofoils – structures that are curved on top but flatter underneath. An aerofoil is angled so that it pushes air downwards, and its shape creates an area of higher pressure below the wing. These two actions create lift.

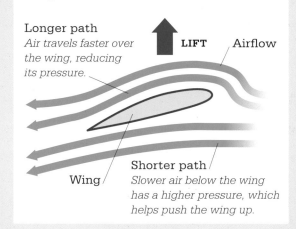

Longer path
Air travels faster over the wing, reducing its pressure.

LIFT

Airflow

Wing

Shorter path
Slower air below the wing has a higher pressure, which helps push the wing up.

Helicopters

The main blades of a helicopter are long aerofoils. Driven by the engine, they spin fast, often at a rate of 300 turns per minute. The speed of the blades and their angle can be altered by the pilot to create more or less lift.

Rotor blades
The main blades are attached to a rotor head. They produce lift as they spin, so the helicopter rises vertically.

Moving forwards
The rotor head tilts so that the blades drive air backwards as well as down.

LIFT

Tail rotor
The rear rotors balance the turning forces created by the main blades.

THRUST

Landing area
Helicopters need only a small space to land, such as on the landing pad of this oil rig.

LIFT

LIFT

Taking off
When a helicopter takes off, there is just an upward lifting force and no forward thrust.

Vertical takeoff
The Sea Harrier is designed to fly from aircraft carriers. It is a VTOL plane, capable of vertical takeoff and landing. Taking off vertically uses a lot of fuel, so the Harrier often takes off conventionally. It speeds along the carrier's flight deck and makes use of a ramp at the end.

Directing thrust
This computer simulation shows how the Harrier's rotating jet-engine nozzles direct their thrust downwards for a vertical takeoff. Once airborne, the nozzles swivel to point behind, pushing the aircraft forwards.

Surface skimmers [Riding

Any boat moving through water is slowed down by a resisting force called drag. Craft that move over the top of the water keep drag to a minimum, so they can travel faster or carry greater loads.

102 kph

(63.5 mph): the top speed of
the Yamaha WaveRunner FX Cruiser

Jet skis

Jet skis are the motorcycles of the water – fast and exciting as they skim the waves. Steered with handlebars, they are pushed along by powerful jets of water. Riders can also lean into turns, just like motorcyclists.

Impeller
This is attached to the drive shaft.

Handlebars

Engine
A petrol engine rapidly spins the drive shaft.

Steering nozzle
The nozzle, turned by the handlebars, alters the direction of thrust.

Water jet

Driveshaft

Intake
Water is drawn in through the duct.

Impeller power
The impeller – a propeller enclosed in a tube called a duct – spins fast to draw in water from under the jet ski. The water is forced out from the nozzle at the rear as a high-pressure jet.

Propeller
A boat's curved, spinning propeller blades force water backwards, which pushes the boat forwards through the water. Aeroplane propellers work in the same way in air.

Mighty machine
The powerful Yamaha WaveRunner FX Cruiser is made of ultra-lightweight but high-strength material. This improves its acceleration and makes it easier to handle. It can carry the driver and two passengers.

the waves]

Hovercraft

These craft are amphibious – able to travel over both water and land. They have fans to generate lift (see page 74) and propellers for thrust. Fins called rudders, positioned in the flow of air behind the propellers, steer the craft.

Cushion of air

The rubber skirt around the base of the hovercraft holds in much of the air pushed underneath by the fans. This lifts the craft off the surface of the water.

Propeller
Pusher propellers at the rear drive the craft forwards.

Lift fan
Large fans driven by the engine push air down with great force.

Flexible rubber skirt

Base of hovercraft

Escaping air
A little bit of air escapes, minimizing friction with the water or ground.

Air cushion
An area of high-pressure air forms under the hovercraft.

Car ferry

In service on the English Channel from 1968 to 2000, the SR.N4 was the biggest-ever commercial hovercraft. It carried up to 416 people and 60 cars.

Hydrofoils

At slow speeds, a hydrofoil travels like a regular boat, with its hull in the water. At high speeds, the hull rises above the surface, supported by winglike foils. A submerged propeller or an impeller (see opposite page) drives the boat along.

Impeller

Rear foil

Lift

Front foil

Water flow

Underwater wings

Like aeroplane wings, the foils under the hull are aerofoils (see page 74). At high speeds, the more rapid flow of water over the curved tops of the foils produces lift, raising the boat's hull out of the water.

Jet-powered hydrofoil

Capable of reaching 84 kph (52 mph), the Boeing 929 Jetfoil is powered not by a propeller but by a water jet, very like a jet ski.

Escaping Earth [Blasting off]

Enormous power is needed to break free of Earth's gravity and head out into space. Rocket launch vehicles use rocket engines that carry their own fuel and oxidizer (source of oxygen). The fuel and oxygen are mixed together and burned to create vast amounts of thrust. The vehicle lifts off when the thrust is greater than the force of gravity pulling down on it.

Space shuttle liftoff
NASA's *Endeavour* space shuttle blasts off on its way to the International Space Station in 2009. The 2 million litres (440,000 gallons) of fuel in the large orange fuel tank were used up during liftoff, so the tank was jettisoned (cast off) just nine minutes after launch.

All shapes and sizes

The first-ever liquid-fuelled rocket was just 3.4 m (11.2 ft) tall and weighed 2.7 kg (6 lb). Modern rockets have to be large enough to carry heavy payloads (cargo such as satellites) and need huge quantities of fuel and oxidizer.

Height in m (ft)

120 (400)

90 (300)

60 (200)

30 (100)

0

Saturn V	Long March	Space shuttle	Ariane 5	Soyuz-FG
USA	China	USA	Europe	Russia
Built 1966	Built 1990	Built 1976	Built 1995–96	Built 2001

Biggest-ever launch vehicles

Saturn V rockets launched all the Apollo missions to the Moon between 1968 and 1972. The rockets stood 110 m (363 ft) tall – 18 m (60 ft) taller than the Statue of Liberty.

Liquid-fuelled rocket

Many rocket engines use a liquid fuel such as hydrogen, petrol, or kerosene. A Saturn V F-1 engine uses 788 kg (1,733 lb) of liquid hydrogen every second.

Intense heat
The rocket engine has to withstand temperatures of up to 3,227°C (5,800°F).

Direction of movement

Fuel tank
Liquid fuel is held under pressure in this tank.

Oxidizer
Giant tanks hold liquid oxygen or another oxygen-generating substance.

Igniter
This system sets light to the fuel and oxygen mixture.

Turbo pumps
High-speed pumps control the flow of fuel and oxidizer.

Combustion chamber
Fuel and oxidizer are burned rapidly here, producing quickly expanding gases.

Direction of thrust

Nozzle
Expanded gases push out of here, creating thrust.

Rocket launch

The heavier the launch vehicle, the more fuel has to be burned to create the thrust needed. One solution is a multistage rocket – each stage (tank) is jettisoned, falling away once its fuel is used up.

Ariane 5
This is a typical launch pattern for the European Space Agency's Ariane 5 rocket.

4 600 seconds
The main engine shuts down and is jettisoned.

3 190–240 seconds
The fairing (which reduces drag) around the upper stage blasts free.

2 130 seconds
The booster rockets are jettisoned, having each burned off 240 tonnes of fuel.

1 Liftoff
Twin solid rocket boosters and the main engine fire.

Space exploration Facts

Launching astronauts in rockets is only one way to explore space. Much of what we know about the Universe comes from telescopes and from robotic space probes that can endure conditions too hostile for humans.

Looking into space

Optical telescopes capture light. Other telescopes gather different forms of energy given off by objects in space, including X-rays and radio waves. Below are some examples of what can be seen from Earth and from telescopes in space. One light-year (ly) is about 9.6 trillion km (6 trillion miles).

2.5 million light-years

Naked eye
The Andromeda galaxy, 2.5 million ly away, is visible by eye on a cloudless night.

54 million light-years

Home telescope
Telescopes reveal more, including M87, a giant galaxy 54 million ly away containing a trillion stars.

600 million light-years

Parkes (radio)
Australia's Parkes telescope has detected radio waves from Cygnus A, a galaxy 600 million ly away.

10.2 billion light-years

Chandra (X-ray)
This orbiting observatory has identified a group of galaxies, JKCS041, around 10.2 billion ly from Earth.

13.2 billion light-years

Hubble (optical)
From its position high above Earth, Hubble has observed the farthest known stars, over 13.2 billion ly away.

Space probes

These unpiloted craft explore the solar system, sending data back to Earth by radio signal. Some fly by their target, measuring it as they go. Others go into orbit around a moon or planet, or even land on it.

SUN — **MERCURY** ● — **VENUS** — **EARTH** — **MARS**

MESSENGER
Target: Mercury (launched 2004)
Distance from Earth: 155 million km (96 million miles) in 2011

Long-distance
Over time, some probes travel vast distances through space.

SMART-1
Target: the Moon (launched 2003)
Distance from Earth: 380,000 km (230,600 miles)

Last men on the Moon
Using their lunar rover, Eugene Cernan and Harrison Schmitt of Apollo 17 collected 111 kg (245 lbs) of Moon rock. They were the last of 12 astronauts who walked on the Moon between 1969 and 1972.

Space junk

Orbiting Earth at an average speed of 28,000 kph (17,400 mph) are millions of bits of debris from space missions. They range from flecks of paint to rocket parts.

Astro-trash
The many items of space junk include a lost camera, glove, and toolkit, as well as rubbish bags.

19,000
pieces of space junk are larger than 10 cm (4 ins)

Space suits

In Earth orbit, spacewalking astronauts face temperatures ranging from −157°C (−250°F) to over 135°C (275°F). They need tough protective suits with built-in life-support systems – and room to grow!

life-support system
The pack includes oxygen tanks, cooling equipment, a radio, and a battery for electrical power.

plastic visor
The visor has a thin gold coating to block the Sun's harmful ultraviolet rays.

Suited and booted
All the suit's parts interlock so that no skin is exposed. The suit weighs about 127 kg (280 lbs) on Earth. However, in space it is weightless.

Growing taller
Without gravity pulling the spine down, the body gets about 5 cm (2 ins) taller.

5cm
4cm
3cm
2cm
1cm

gloves
Heated fingertips keep fingers from going numb while working in space.

layers
The suit has 14 layers. Some keep the body at the right temperature. Others protect against tiny space rocks called micrometeoroids.

Asteroid belt

JUPITER   SATURN   URANUS   NEPTUNE   PLUTO

New Horizons
Target: Pluto (launched 2006)
Distance from Earth: 4.8 billion km
(3 billion miles) in 2015

Rosetta
Target: Comet 67P (launched 2004)
Distance from Earth: 654 million km (406 million miles) in 2014

Pioneer 10
Target: Jupiter (launched 1972)
Distance from Earth: 12 billion km (7.5 billion miles)

Voyager 1
Target: deep space (launched 1977)
Distance from Earth: 17.4 billion km (10.8 billion miles)

Construction in space

The International Space Station (ISS) is an orbiting base for scientific research. It is 109 m (358 ft) long and circles Earth more than 15 times a day, 354 kilometres (220 miles) above the planet's surface.

1998 The first module, Russia's Zarya – used for communications, power, and storage – was launched.

2000 With living quarters and a control centre fitted, the ISS received its first full-time crew of three astronauts.

2001 The Destiny science lab was added.

2002 The P1 and S1 parts of the truss – the ISS's giant spine – were fitted.

INSIDE KIBO LABORATORY

2008 The ISS gained a Japanese laboratory, Kibo, a European science module called Columbus, and Dextre, a giant, twin-armed Canadian robot.

2011 *Atlantis* made the 115th and final space shuttle visit to the ISS.

VIEW OF THE ISS IN 2011

2012 The ISS is scheduled to be complete and capable of running until 2020.

> "This space station is the **pinnacle of human achievement and** international cooperation."
> —GREG CHAMITOFF, ISS ASTRONAUT

Techn

for

* What is a solar furnace?

* When were the first colour TV broadcasts?

* How do trainers put an extra spring in your step?

ology
life

Mountain bike [Pedal power!]

Some bicycles are designed for cruising smooth city streets or riding along country lanes. But others, like this rugged mountain bike, give you the freedom to go off-road and tackle almost any terrain. Mountain bikes are built with specially designed materials that can withstand the jolts of a ride over rough ground.

"Penny-farthing" bicycles
Early bikes had no chain or gears, and the pedals were connected to the front wheel. The large wheel (the "penny") gave a smooth ride on uneven roads, steadied by the smaller "farthing".

On your bike

This lightweight mountain bike has full suspension, meaning that both the front and back wheels have suspension systems. It is designed to be ridden on bumpy trails or raced on off-road courses that have hills, dips, rocks, and other obstacles.

Rear suspension
The air chamber acts like a spring, absorbing the force of hitting a bump. The oil and nitrogen chambers dampen the piston's movement as it returns to normal.

Nitrogen chamber

Air chamber

Oil chamber

Floating piston

Rubber tread
The chunky tread is designed to grip rough ground.

Beads
Metal or Kevlar rings called beads help to give the tyre its shape.

Subtread
This tough inner layer protects the tyre against punctures.

Disc brakes
When activated, pads press hard against a disc on the wheel. This creates friction, which slows down the wheel.

Rear fork

Downhill racing
On steep slopes, mountain bikes can reach over 80 kph (50 mph).

Saddle
The seat is cushioned with gel pads to make the ride as comfortable as possible.

Lightweight frame
With carbon-fibre or aluminium-alloy frames, some mountain bikes weigh less than 10.9 kg (24 lb).

Gear derailleur
This mechanism directs the chain over the cog selected when the rider operates the gearshift.

Aluminium wheel and spokes

Gear shift

Rear suspension

Handlebars

Brake lever
This lever operates the hydraulic (pressurized-liquid) braking system.

Front suspension

Front suspension
Supported by springs, these tubes move up and down to cushion the rider over rough ground.

Air valve

Air chamber

Air piston

Spring

Lubrication oil

Lights
These contain several small but very bright light-emitting diode (LED) lamps to make a cyclist visible at night.

1.5 billion: the estimated number of bicycles on the world's roads in 2011

Gear cogs
The gear cassette on the rear wheel of this bike has ten different gear cogs, known as sprockets.

Bearings
These reduce friction.

Chainwheel

Crank

Chain and chainwheel
The chain connects the chainwheel to the cogs and transmits power from the pedals to the wheel.

MTB pedals
Mountain bike (MTB) shoes can be clipped into the pedals, allowing riders to generate power throughout the entire pedalling motion.

Head protection
A helmet reduces the chances of injuring your head if you crash. Most helmets consist of a hard plastic outer shell with a layer of thick expanded polystyrene foam inside.

Cool air in

Hard shell

The chin strap keeps the helmet in place.

Warm air out

Air vents
Holes channel air around a cyclist's head to keep it cool.

Structure
The crushable foam layer under the outer shell cushions the head. It absorbs much of the force of an impact.

Foam layer

Plastic outer shell

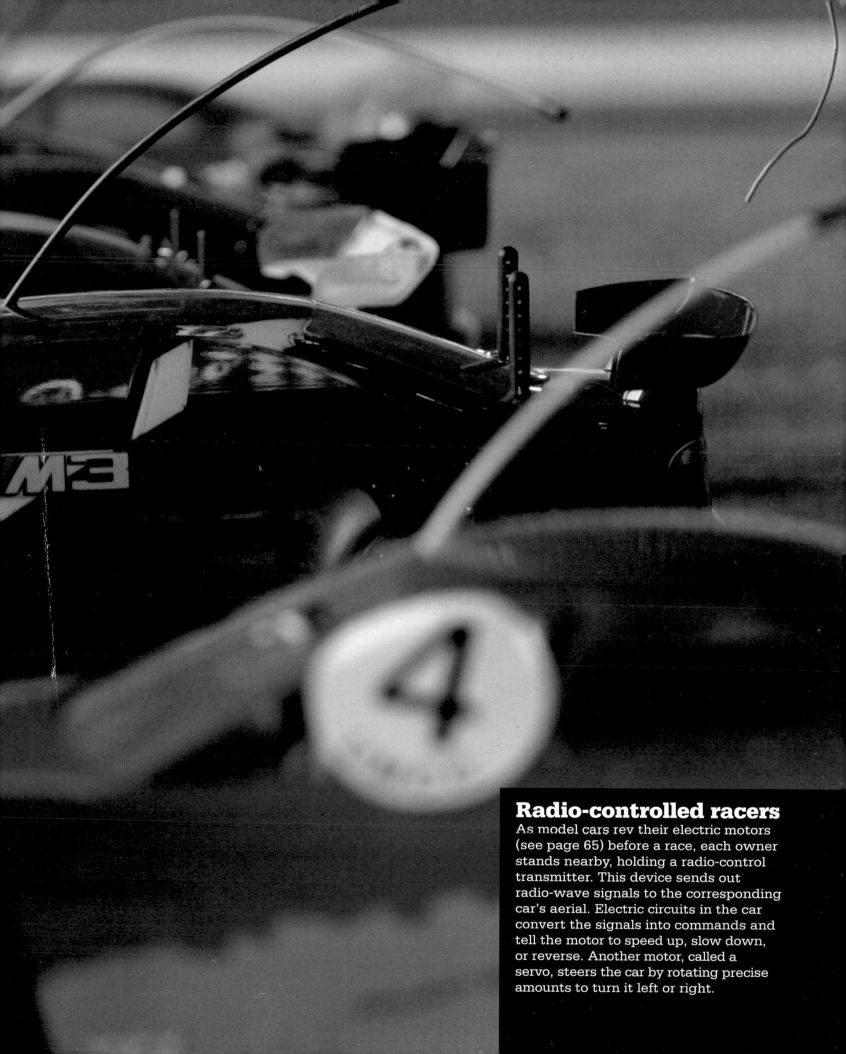

Radio-controlled racers

As model cars rev their electric motors (see page 65) before a race, each owner stands nearby, holding a radio-control transmitter. This device sends out radio-wave signals to the corresponding car's aerial. Electric circuits in the car convert the signals into commands and tell the motor to speed up, slow down, or reverse. Another motor, called a servo, steers the car by rotating precise amounts to turn it left or right.

Much of the energy that heats and lights our homes and powers our gadgets comes from burning fossil fuels (coal, oil, and gas). This creates pollution and releases carbon dioxide gas (CO_2), which is a cause of climate change. Saving energy reduces pollution, CO_2 in the air, and energy bills.

New gadgets

Many domestic electrical devices, such as PCs and game consoles, did not exist 30 years ago. Today, the amount of electricity that game consoles use in the USA could power the city of San Diego, California.

Rapid change

In 1978, many homes had washing machines, but big flat-screen TVs and DVD players had not yet been invented.

OWNERSHIP IN US HOMES

	2009	1978
WASHING MACHINE	82%	74%
TV SET OVER 35"	45%	0%
DVD PLAYER	79%	0%

World energy use

From 1900 to 2000, with the introduction of lots of new technology, the world's energy use increased by more than 10 times. However, the amount of energy used by people in different countries varies greatly.

India 545
China 1,598
United Kingdom 3,197
Germany 3,893
France 3,920
Australia 5,975
United States 7,075

ANNUAL ENERGY USE PER PERSON, IN KILOGRAMS

Annual energy use

On average, each US citizen consumes nearly 13 times more energy than someone living in India.

KEY

= 1 BARREL, OR 350 KG (770 LB), OF OIL, OR EQUIVALENT

GAS 24.2%
OIL 37.2%
COAL 19.7%

Nuclear power 11.3%
Hydroelectricity 2.1%
Combustible renewables and waste 4.4%
Other: wind, solar, and geothermal power 1.1%

Energy sources

Over 80 per cent of the world's energy comes from the fossil fuels coal, oil, and natural gas, but they won't last forever.

Running out

The world is gradually using up its known reserves of coal, oil, and gas. Below are possible cutoff dates, if consumption does not lessen and no new reserves are found.

2055	2072	2128
OIL	NATURAL GAS	COAL

An average house in the US uses
30.16 kWh
of electricity each day

Device	Photovoltaic panel
What it does	Sunlight makes electricity flow in the panel

Device	Wind turbine
What it does	Wind spins the blades, generating current

Device	Solar heating tube
What it does	Sunlight heats water in the tube

Helping the planet

We can reduce consumption of fossil fuels by using more energy-efficient devices, unplugging unused appliances, and installing technology that harnesses alternative energy sources, such as sunlight and wind (see pages 100–103).

Alternative energy technology

Photovoltaic panels and wind turbines supply electricity for use in the home, while solar heating tubes provide hot water. All three devices are usually attached to roofs.

60 W

13–15 W

6–8 W

TRADITIONAL INCANDESCENT BULB

COMPACT FLUORESCENT LAMP (CFL)

LIGHT-EMITTING DIODE (LED) BULB

Comparing light-bulb efficiency

Different bulbs of the same brightness have different power ratings (see right). LED bulbs use up to 10 times less electricity than incandescent ones.

If every US home replaced one incandescent bulb with a CFL, the energy saved could light 3 million houses

ELECTRIC KETTLE
2,000 W

Power ratings

The higher a device's power rating in watts (W) is, the more electricity it uses. Some devices use electricity even when they are in standby mode.

HAIR DRYER
1,000 W

25" COLOUR TV
150 W

VIDEO GAME CONSOLE
80–90 W

Wattages

Our domestic appliances have a wide range of power ratings. Those that heat water or air tend to use more electricity.

TABLE FAN
25 W

ELECTRIC SHAVER
15 W

WASHING MACHINE
500 W

Domestic tech [A helping

Technology has transformed domestic life, bringing heat, light, new methods of preserving and preparing food, and entertainment to our homes. It has also given us labour-saving devices, such as dishwashers and vacuum cleaners, that help make daily tasks less of a chore.

1876
Telephone
In Boston, USA, Alexander Graham Bell, a Scottish-born inventor, made the first telephone voice call. Later the same year, he made the first two-way long-distance phone call.

EARLY BELL TELEPHONE, 1877

c.100 BCE
Central heating
The ancient Romans invented an underfloor central heating system called a hypocaust. Hot air from a furnace warmed rooms as it passed through gaps in the walls and spaces below the raised floors.

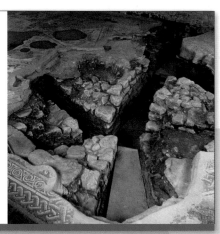

UNDERFLOOR HEATING AT A ROMAN VILLA

1902
In the USA, Willis Haviland Carrier built the first electric air-conditioning system. It was installed in a printing factory.

1909
The first commercially successful electric toaster is patented in the USA by Frank Shailor.

Dots represent 10-year increases.

100 BCE 1500 1870

Dots represent 100-year increases.

c.3000–2700 BCE
Plumbing pipes to carry water to and from houses were developed by the Indus Valley civilization (in modern-day Pakistan).

c.710 BCE
The oldest known lock and key were installed at the palace of Sargon II, ruler of Assyria (now part of Iraq).

1886
Josephine Cochrane of Ohio, USA, designed a mechanical dishwasher to keep her servants from breaking crockery when washing up.

Carbon filament

1596
Flushing toilet
Sir John Harrington, the godson of Queen Elizabeth I of England, designed and installed a flushing mechanical "water closet", or toilet, in his manor house at Kelston, Somerset.

DIAGRAM OF JOHN HARRINGTON'S TOILET

1878–79
Electric lightbulb
American inventor Thomas Edison developed the first commercially successful lightbulb. A filament (thin strand) of carbon glowed with light when electricity passed through it.

EDISON'S FILAMENT LIGHTBULB, 1879

340 kg (750 lbs)
– the weight of the very first microwave oven, the Raytheon Radarange

1954
Colour television
The United States became the first country to have nationwide colour TV broadcasts, and many electronics companies began selling colour sets.

FERGUSON 306T TELEVISION, UK, 1956

FAMILY VIEWING, 1950s

1929
The first electric razor, invented by Colonel Jacob Schick, went on sale in the USA.

1947
The US company Raytheon launched the first microwave oven, which stood more than 1.8 m (6 feet) tall.

1955
In the USA, Eugene Polley designed the first wireless TV remote control, the Zenith Flash-Matic.

2011
LG developed a smart fridge that connects to the Internet. Owners can check its contents by phone while out shopping.

• •1930 •1940 • • • • •2000 • •

1927
American J. W. Hammes built a waste disposal system that ground up food waste so it could be flushed down a drain.

1956
French couple Marc and Colette Grégoire made the first non-stick pans, which were coated with a slippery material called Teflon.

2010
3D TV sets, made by Panasonic, Samsung, and LG, became widely available in stores in the USA and UK.

1922
Electric blender
Stephen Poplawski, a Polish-born American, invented the blender, which uses spinning blades to liquefy food. Many stores bought his machine to make drinks such as milk shakes.

EARLY ELECTRIC BLENDER

1983
Cyclonic vacuum
After five years of testing and more than 5,000 prototypes, British industrial designer James Dyson built the first cyclonic vacuum cleaner, the G-Force. Cyclonic vacuums use swirling air to capture dust and dirt. Previously, all vacuums contained bags to collect dust.

DYSON WITH HIS 2005 BALL VACUUM CLEANER

JAMES DYSON
British inventor

Founded:	Dyson Ltd.
Invented:	Cyclonic vacuum

Sports shoe [Get a grip!]

A modern athletic shoe is a miracle of modern engineering. Designed by computer, dozens of different materials are glued, stitched, or fitted together with precision.

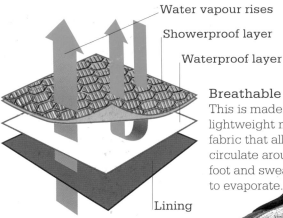

Water vapour rises

Showerproof layer

Waterproof layer

Breathable upper
This is made of a lightweight mesh fabric that allows air to circulate around the foot and sweat to evaporate.

Lining

Laces
Laces are made of 40 or more individual cotton or polyester threads woven together by machine.

Vintage soccer boot
This 1930s soccer boot made from thick leather got heavier when it became wet. Screw-in studs made of plastic and rubber– for gripping the turf – were introduced in the 1950s.

Running shoe

A modern running shoe needs to protect and support a runner's foot yet still be lightweight. As many as 20 cutting-edge materials may make up a single shoe, radically reducing the weight. Some shoes weigh as little as (142–198 g (5–7 oz) each.

Breathable upper

Toe bumper
Made of moulded rubber or plastic, this adds protection to the front of the shoe and prevents stubbed toes.

Cushioned insole
This is cut out of sheets of polyurethane foam and often treated with chemicals to neutralize foot odour.

Midsole
Often made of moulded plastic, this gives the shoe its shape and supports the arch of your foot.

Gel pad

Foot impact

The pad absorbs some impact.

Gel pad
A pad of silicon gel helps absorb the shock when the ball of your foot strikes the ground.

Force spreads outwards.

Tongue
The foam for this is made by injecting millions of tiny air bubbles into a plastic liquid and letting it set.

Ankle support
Made of soft plastic foam to cushion your heel, this keeps you from slipping out of the shoe.

Reflective strips

Reflective strips
Tiny plastic prisms reflect 80 per cent of light and make runners safely visible at night.

VIEW FROM ABOVE

Light out   Light in

SIDE VIEW

Heel cushion
This springy moulded foam spreads the impact as your heel strikes the ground.

Hard-wearing tread
The rubber-based tread can grip wet, slippery surfaces.

Biomechanics
The study of how your body moves is called biomechanics. Footwear makers use it to help them design better sports shoes. Running is a repetitive set of movements, with several thousand steps taken for every hour of exercise.

Impact pressure
Pressure sensors can measure the impact of your weight on the soles of your feet. This colour-coded image shows different levels of pressure, with red areas having the most.

Recording data
High-speed cameras can capture the positions of athletes' feet, ankles, and legs as they leave the starting blocks and get into their running stride. These images are used to determine the forces and strains on the foot and the shoe.

$2.42
billion: the amount spent on running and jogging shoes in the USA in 2010

Human engineering

Health technology already assists many people. They may use motorized wheelchairs, hearing aids, prostheses (artificial body parts), and artificial implants to replace failing or missing parts. In the future, technology may replace more and more of the human body.

Human upgrade

Some futuristic films feature cyborgs – beings that are part human and part machine, with technology that gives them abilities superior to ordinary people. Although cyborgs are fictional, some artificial body parts being built today can match or even outperform their natural equivalents.

Film cyborg
In *The Terminator* (1984), a powerful cyborg is sent back in time from 2029.

Hand

I-limb ultra
High-tech artificial hands, such as the i-limb ultra, offer realistic movement. They use touch and force sensors to adjust the strength of their grip. The i-limb ultra can carry a load of up to 90 kg (198.4 lb).

Skin

Made in the laboratory
New skin can be made by growing skin cells over a framework built of collagen, a protein found in body tissues. Scientists hope to be able to interweave artificial nerve fibres into the skin to give it the sense of touch.

Artificial skin grows over an ear-shaped structure.

Chip

Microchip implants
One day, a microchip under the skin may be able to send radio signals to confirm a person's identity or inform doctors of a patient's medical conditions. Some chips might even run GPS (see pages 30–31), enabling rescuers to find lost people.

Each finger moves independently.

Eye

Argus II

This system restores some sight to blind or partially sighted people. It uses a camera mounted on spectacles to relay video signals to electrodes in an implant in the eye. The electrodes then send electrical signals to the brain via the optic nerve.

EYE IMPLANT

Tiny electrodes

An antenna communicates with the camera.

Flex-Foot

The Flex-Foot Cheetah is a carbon-fibre prosthetic lower leg and foot. It squashes and bends as it lands, then springs back into shape to drive the runner forward.

Spring power

South African sprinter Oscar Pistorius uses a Flex-Foot on each leg when he runs in races.

Opening for blood flow

Heart

AbioCor implant

The AbioCor, a complete replacement heart, pumps up to 12 litres (2.5 gallons) of blood around the body per minute. It is powered by a battery pack, worn on the hip, and an implanted rechargeable battery.

AbioCor contains a motor-driven hydraulic pumping system.

Hip

Artificial ball-and-socket joint

The dish-like socket fits into the pelvis, and the ball joint attaches to the femur (thigh bone). Hip replacement operations often use a robot to drill accurately into the patient's femur so that the prosthetic can be fitted.

The metal ball fits into the socket in the pelvis.

The plastic body fits into the femur.

Nanorobots

One day, doctors may be able to inject microscopic devices called nanorobots into the body. Once inside, nanorobots could clear blood vessels of fatty deposits, repair damaged tissues, monitor health, and release medicines.

Faster than the wind

In 2009, in California, USA, the Ecotricity Greenbird achieved a speed of 203.1 kph (126.2 mph) – a world record for a wind-powered land vehicle. Built of carbon-fibre materials, the Greenbird is a land yacht. Unlike other land yachts, it uses a solid vertical wing instead of a cloth sail to harness the wind and propel itself forward over ice or dry lake beds.

Wind and waves [Power from

Using technology, we can harness the energy of rushing winds and crashing waves to generate electricity. Like solar power (see pages 102–103), these pollution-free energy sources will never run out.

Mills and pumps

The ancient Chinese and Babylonians first used windmills to grind wheat and other grains into flour more than 2,000 years ago. Other early wind-powered machines pumped water up from wells. Wind pumps are still used today on farms and in isolated places.

Greek windmill
Gears transmit the sails' turning motion to large, round grinding stones.

Anemometer
This measures the wind speed.

Gearbox

Shaft

Brake

Blade

Controller

Generator

Nose cone

Motor

Tower

Inside a turbine
The turbine has a motor as well as a generator. The motor swings the turbine around so that it points into the wind.

Power cable

Wind turbines

Horizontal-axis wind turbines have propeller-like blades. As the blades rotate in the wind, they spin a shaft that drives a generator. The electricity produced supplies factories, offices, and homes. Producing electricity from wind power avoids using up the world's limited supplies of fossil fuels (see page 90).

Offshore wind farm
Perched on top of tall towers at sea or on land, wind turbines grouped together in clusters are called wind farms.

5,000:
the number of homes
that can be powered by an ENERCON E-126 wind turbine

nature]

Types of turbine

A turbine's power depends on its location and size. Large horizontal-axis turbines, such as the huge ENERCON E-126, are the most powerful. Vertical-axis designs, such as helical, Darrieus, and Savonius turbines, are easier to build since they can be placed closer to the ground.

Horizontal axis
This needs to point into the wind to work.

Helical-Darrieus
This works when wind gusts from all directions.

Darrieus
This spins when air catches its two blades.

Savonius
This is mounted on a rotating shaft.

Harnessing waves

In an oscillating water column system, such as the LIMPET on the Scottish island of Islay, the advance and retreat of ocean waves push air past a special set of blades called a Wells turbine. The rotation of the turbine drives a generator that produces electricity.

Islay LIMPET
This device produces enough electricity to power 400 homes.

1 Water in
As the waves break, water flows into a chamber. The water pushes air out, spinning the Wells turbine's blades.

Air out
The turbine spins as air is forced out.

2 Water out
When the water recedes, air is sucked into the chamber. The air flows over the turbine and spins its blades once again.

Air in
As it enters, air spins the turbine.

Solar power [Energy from

The Sun sends out huge amounts of energy. Some of it reaches Earth and warms the planet, allowing life to flourish. The Sun's energy can also help generate power without burning fossil fuels (coal, oil, and natural gas) and creating pollution.

Nieuwland roof tiles

Over 500 homes in Nieuwland, the Netherlands, have roofs made of photovoltaic panels rather than roof tiles. Together, they generate 1.35 million watts of power.

Built by	REMU and the city of Amersfoort, the Netherlands
Used for	Providing electricity to schools and homes
Introduced	1995

Rooftop providers
The roof panels supply enough power to meet most of each home's electricity needs.

PlanetSolar

The top of this boat is covered with 537 sq m (5,780 sq ft) of photovoltaic panels, each one a collection of cells (see below). The electricity they produce powers motors that turn the boat's propellers.

Built by	Knierim Yacht Club, Kiel, Germany
Used for	Travelling around the world by solar-powered boat
Introduced	2010

Cruising the ocean
The twin-hulled, 31-m (102-ft) *PlanetSolar* has a maximum speed of 26 kph (16 mph).

Photovoltaic cell

In a photovoltaic (PV) cell, sunlight knocks negatively charged particles called electrons off atoms. The electrons then flow as an electric current.

Inside a PV cell
There are two layers of semiconductor material sandwiched between electrically charged plates.

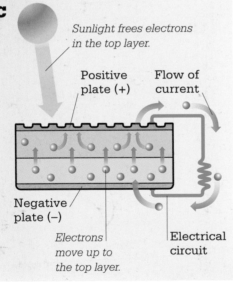

Sunlight frees electrons in the top layer.

Positive plate (+)

Flow of current

Negative plate (−)

Electrons move up to the top layer.

Electrical circuit

Converter pack

The small photovoltaic panels on the Converter Solar Backpack can be used to recharge a device stored inside, such as a mobile phone or an MP3 player. An hour of sunlight gives a phone enough power for two to three hours of talk time.

Built by	Voltaic Systems, USA
Used for	Recharging the batteries of small electrical devices
Introduced	2004

Power pack
Each of the two PV panels provides 2 watts of power.

NLV Quant

The experimental Quant car has electric motors (see page 65) rather than a petrol engine. The car is coated with a thin photovoltaic film, which converts sunlight into electricity to drive the motors.

Built by	NLV Solar AG, Switzerland
Used for	Driving with solar power at up to 377 kph (234 mph)
Introduced	2012

NLV QUANT

PHOTOVOLTAIC PYRITE FILM

Mineral coating
The film is made from the mineral pyrite, also known as fool's gold.

sunlight]

Odeillo furnace

Solar furnaces use mirrors to concentrate the energy of the Sun's rays onto a small area. The intense heat generated can be used to melt metals or turn water into steam for driving electricity generators.

Built by	National Centre for Scientific Research, Odeillo, France
Used for	Testing metals and other materials; generating electricity
Introduced	1970

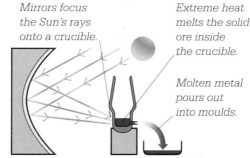

Mirrors focus the Sun's rays onto a crucible.

Extreme heat melts the solid ore inside the crucible.

Molten metal pours out into moulds.

Metal from ore

Solar furnaces can produce metals from ores (rocks that contain metal) without using a lot of electricity.

3,500°C (6,330°F):
the maximum temperature reached at the Odeillo solar furnace

Reflecting dish

Odeillo uses 63 flat mirrors arranged in a dish shape to focus sunlight on the central tower containing the crucible.

Eco-city, day and night

Masdar City, in the United Arab Emirates, will be home to 50,000 people when it is completed in 2016. It will produce most of its energy at solar-power plants and recycle almost all of its waste. No petrol-powered cars will be allowed in the city. Instead, people will walk or use pod cars – small vehicles that run on solar electricity. During the day (left), the main square will be shaded by giant parasols that capture energy from sunlight. At night (right), the parasols will fold up and release the collected energy as heat.

MASDAR CITY, UNITED ARAB EMIRATES

Acceleration
The increase in speed of an object.

Accelerometer
A sensor that detects and measures movement.

Aerodynamics
The study of how air passes over and around objects. Aerodynamics research can help vehicles such as aircraft and cars move through air more smoothly, to travel faster or use less fuel.

Aerofoil
A wing-shaped device that generates the force of lift when it travels through air.

Altitude
The height above sea or ground level of an object in space or Earth's atmosphere.

Amplification
The increase in the loudness of a sound.

App
A computer program that performs a task, such as entering text or playing a sound file. *App* is short for *application*.

Artificial intelligence
The science and study of building machines with the ability to learn and think in human-like ways.

Autonomous
Having the ability to make decisions and work alone without a human supervisor, as some robots can.

Bit
The smallest unit of computer memory that can be represented by an electrical signal as on or off. Eight bits make up a byte. *Bit* is short for *binary digit*.

Blog
An updatable webpage used as a diary or journal, available for others to read on the World Wide Web. *Blog* is short for *web log*.

Bluetooth
A wireless communications system that uses radio waves to transmit data over short distances.

Bug
A hidden device, used by spies, that usually contains a microphone and a transmitter. Bugs secretly collect and transmit conversations and other sounds.

Catalytic converter
A device in a motor vehicle that removes some of the harmful polluting chemicals in the gases emitted by the vehicle's engine.

Circuit board
A sheet of insulating material on which components in electronic equipment are mounted.

Client
A computer or other device in a computer network that requests information.

Combustion
The chemical reaction between a fuel and oxygen that produces heat and, usually, light.

Controller
The part of a robot that receives information from its sensors and makes decisions about how to control the rest of the robot.

CPU
A microprocessor that controls many of the functions of a computer. *CPU* stands for *central processing unit*.

Digital
Operating with data or information in numerical form. Modern computers use digital processing techniques.

Drag
The resistance that a vehicle or other moving object experiences when it travels through air. This force slows the object down.

Electromagnet
A form of magnet that can be switched on and off. When it is turned on, electricity flows through a coil of wire, creating a magnetic field.

End effector
A tool, such as a paint-spraying gun or gripping hand, that can be attached to a robot so that it is able to perform a task.

Exabyte (EB)
A unit of computer memory storage space that is equal to 1 quintillion bytes.

Gigabyte (GB)
A unit of computer memory storage space that is equal to 1,024 megabytes (MB).

GPS
A satellite system orbiting Earth that tells users their exact location and the correct time. *GPS* stands for *Global Positioning System.*

Gravity
The force that pulls objects together. Gravity causes objects to be pulled towards a planet.

Hybrid vehicle
A motor vehicle that has both an internal combustion engine and a rechargeable motor or energy system to reduce fuel use.

Hydraulic
Moved or operated by pressurized liquid in tubes.

Inclinometer
A sensor that measures the angles of slopes.

Internet
A global network that connects computers worldwide and allows them to communicate by sending information in small units.

Internet traffic
The amount of data sent via the Internet.

IT
The industry that is concerned with computing. *IT* stands for *information technology.*

More than 1 billion transistors are made every second

Glossary

Kilobyte (KB)
A unit of computer memory that is equal to 1,024 bytes.

LED
A small device that shines light when powered by electricity. *LED* stands for *light-emitting diode.*

Lenticular lens
A curved lens that allows each eye to see a different image of the same object at exactly the same time.

Lift
The force needed to raise an object such as a plane or spacecraft into the air and keep it from falling.

Light-year (ly)
A unit equal to the distance that light can travel in one year in empty space. A light-year is approximately 9.5 trillion km (5.9 trillion miles).

Megabyte (MB)
A unit of computer memory storage space that is equal to 1,024 kilobytes (KB).

Microchip
A collection of microscopic electronic circuits on a small piece of semiconductor material such as silicon.

Microphone
A device that converts sound waves into electrical signals that can be recorded or amplified.

Microprocessor
A computer processor consisting of microscopic electronic circuits and components contained on a single wafer of silicon.

Micro-surgery
Internal surgery that uses tiny tools and cameras to give the surgeon a good view inside the body.

A NeXT computer used by Tim Berners-Lee was the world's first web server

Motherboard
The main circuit board in a personal computer, containing many of its key parts, including its central processing unit (CPU).

MTSO
A computer system that tracks phone calls and their locations, transfers calls between cells, and monitors the length and cost of calls. *MTSO* stands for *Mobile Telephone Switching Office.*

Nanotechnology
The science of building machines and robots in tiny sizes measured in nanometers. A nanometer is a billionth of a metre.

Network
A connection between two or more computers that enables them to communicate.

Operating system
A program or collection of programs that manages a computer or smartphone's resources and parts. Apple iOS, Windows 7, and Android are all common operating systems.

Particle accelerator
A machine that uses magnets to accelerate particles around a track. Collisions between the particles release huge amounts of energy and sometimes create new particles or new elements.

Photovoltaic cell
A small device, made of multiple layers, that produces electricity when light shines on its surface.

Pneumatic
Filled with air, or moved or operated by pressurized air in tubes.

Propeller
A set of blades that spin in air or water to make a vehicle move.

Prototype
An early model of a new product – usually full size and operational – that is designed for testing or publicity.

RAM
The memory space used by a computer to perform calculations and tasks or for storage of data. *RAM* stands for *random-access memory.*

Robotics
The branch of science and technology that develops machines that perform tasks automatically.

Rocket
A missile or vehicle that is propelled by the combustion of a fuel and a contained oxygen supply. A rocket ejects gases to thrust the vehicle forwards or upwards.

ROM
The memory space used by a computer to permanently store program instructions, operating procedures, or other data. *ROM* stands for *read-only memory.*

Rotor blade
A long, thin aerofoil that spins to generate lift to support a helicopter in the air.

Satellite
An object that orbits a planet or another body. Satellites can be natural, such as the Moon, or made by people, such as communications satellites that relay TV pictures around Earth.

Search engine
A giant database of websites that can be searched and accessed by users on the Internet.

Semiconductor
A material whose electrical conductivity is between that of a metal and a nonmetal. Silicon is a semiconductive material that is used in many different technologies.

Sensor
A device that can detect (and sometimes measure) aspects of its surroundings, such as heat, light, and movement.

Server
A computer that relays data or resources to client computers in a computer network.

SIM card
A small card with a microchip that holds cell phone data, such as phone numbers. *SIM* stands for *subscriber identity module.*

Simulator

A machine or computer program that models, or simulates, a real-life situation—such as flying an aircraft—for research or training.

SMS

A system that allows mobile phones to send and receive text messages of up to 160 characters. *SMS* stands for *Short Message Service.*

Software

Programs that instruct a computer how to operate and perform tasks.

Space probe

A scientific machine sent into space by rocket or shuttle to travel past or land on planets, moons, and other objects in space and investigate them.

Stereoscopic 3D

A system that uses two images, one for each eye, to create a 3D effect.

Suspension

A system of springs, shock absorbers, and other components directly connected to the wheels or axles of a vehicle that affects its handling.

Tablet

A type of computing device, such as the iPad or Galaxy Tab, that uses a flat touch-screen display.

Telescope

An instrument used to observe distant objects by collecting and focusing their electromagnetic radiation. Optical telescopes observe visible light, and radio telescopes detect radio waves.

Thrust

The force, usually generated by an engine, that pushes a vehicle forward.

Touchscreen

An input device for computers or mobile phones that displays options on a flat screen. Options are selected by touching the screen.

Transistor

A small electronic switch that replaced much larger and less reliable vacuum tubes in electric circuitry. Transistors have helped make smaller, more powerful electronic technology possible.

Velocity

The measurement of the speed of an object when it is moving in a particular direction.

Virtual world

A computer-generated simulation of a three-dimensional (3D) environment. Users are able to experience and interact with images in a virtual world.

VTOL

The ability of some aircraft to rise straight up into the air without rolling along a runway to generate lift. *VTOL* stands for *vertical takeoff and landing.*

Website

A collection of pages or screens full of information that are made available to users over the World Wide Web.

Wi-Fi

A system that uses radio signals to allow computers and other devices to transmit and receive data over distances of up to a few hundred metres.

World Wide Web

The part of the Internet that contains a series of documents and resources linked together and viewed by a web browser.

APPLE iPAD TABLET

A

AbroCor heart implant 97
acceleration 66
aerofoil 74, 77
aeroplane 64–65, 70, 74–75
aerofoils 74, 77
Airbus A380 74
Antonov An-225 74
Flyer 74
air-conditioning 92
Airbus A380 74
Amazon.com website 29
amplifier 41
analogue signal 18, 26, 54, 55
analytical engine 24
Android operating system 20, 22, 46
Angry Birds game 46
Antonov An-225 74
app 20, 23
games 23
iPhone 23
navigation 23
social networking 23
sounds 23
texting 23
travel 23
Apple iOS operating system 20, 22, 46
Apollo 17 mission 80
arcade game 44, 45
Ariane 5 rocket 79
Argos satellite system 28
Argus II eye implant 97
Armstrong, Billie-Joe 56
artificial implants 96
artificial skin 96
Aston Martin DB5 34
astronaut 80, 81, 82, 83
Cernan, Eugene 80
Schmitt, Harrison 80
Atari 44
Atari 2600 games console 44, 46

Atlantis space shuttle 83
auction, online 29
Autom robot 41
autonomous underwater vehicle (AUV) 40
Autosub3 40

B

Babbage, Charles 24
analytical engine 24
Baer, Ralph 44
battery 14, 19, 48
lithium-ion 21, 48, 69
rechargeable 19, 21, 25, 49, 97
Battlezone game 44
Bell, Alexander Graham 92
Benz, Karl 68
bicycle 86–89
see also mountain bike
penny-farthing 86
bit 18
BlackBerry 5810 mobile phone 15
BlackBerry operating system 22
blender, electric 92
blogging 29
Bluetooth 18, 47
Boeing 777-300ER aircraft 65
Bond, James 34
Brown Box games console 44
bug (listening device) 34
Bugatti Veyron 66–67
computer-controlled 66
parts of 66–67
suspension 66, 67
turbocharger 66

C

calculator 24
camcorder 48–49
autofocus 49

camera 14, 35, 36, 48, 50
digital 21, 41, 48–49, 50
digital signal processor (DSP) 48
filter 48
polarizing 51
UV 48
hard disk 48
lens 48, 50
lenticule 51
memory card 49
MINOX 35
playback 49
sensor 48
still 48
Canadarm2 robot 40
car 63, 66–69, 102
airbag 69
anti-lock braking system (ABS) 69
Aston Martin DB5 34
Bugatti Veyron 66–67
catalytic converter 69
electric ignition 68
fastest 69
Ferrari F40 69
hybrid 69
mass-produced 68
Model-T Ford 68
monster truck 69
Motorwagen 68
Nissan LEAF 69
phone 14
Pod 104
seat belt 68
Smart Car 69
tyre 66, 68
Volkswagen "Beetle" 68
Carrier, Willis Havilland 92
cassette 54
cat's eye road stud 68
CD 18, 55
central heating 92
central processing unit (CPU) 17, 19
arithmetic logic unit

(ALU) 19
control unit 19
Chapman, Anna 35
codes 34
Colossus computer 24
computer 17, 18–19, 20, 21, 24–25, 26–27, 29, 35, 36, 49, 61, 66, 94
see also central processing unit, laptop, supercomputer
Colossus 24
Deep Blue 25
design 94
ENIAC 24
first portable 25
hard-disk drive 18
home 44
Macintosh (Mac) 18–19, 25
motherboard 17, 19
NeXT 107
Nimrod 44
operating system 18, 20
Android 20, 46
Apple iOS 20, 46
Symbian 20, 46
Windows 25
program 18, 19, 20, 21, 23, 37, 44–45
random access memory (RAM) 18, 19, 21
read-only memory (ROM) 19
register 19
server 26–27
storage 19
UNIVAC 1 24
computer network 27
client 27
Cooper, Martin 14
crash-test dummy 68
Sierra Sam 68
Cray-1 supercomputer 25
Cyber Command, USA 35
cyborg 96

D

da Vinci robot 40
Dance Central game 47
Dance Dance Revolution game 45
Darrieus wind turbine 101
data centre 26–27
data processing 18, 19, 20, 22–23, 26–27
Deep Blue computer 25
Diddy Kong game 46
dishwasher 92
disk 18, 24
digital 18, 26, 48, 54
downloads 55
images 48
signal 18, 26, 54
Donkey Kong game 44
drag *see* force
DVD 18, 55
Dyson, James 93

E

eBay 29
eco-city 104–105
Ecotricity Greenbird land yacht 98–99
Edison, Thomas 92
electric charge 20, 21, 89
electric field 20
electrical signal 22, 23, 26, 48
electricity 21, 65, 100, 101, 102, 104
electron 8, 21
Elizabeth I, Queen of England 92
email 15, 20, 26, 28–29
first 24
Endeavour space shuttle 78
ENERCON E-126 wind turbine 100–101
energy 64
electrical 64
fossil fuel 90–91

nuclear 90
solar 90–91, 101, 102
wind 100–101
engine 63, 64–65, 66–67, 69, 70, 72, 102
internal combustion 64, 66–67
jet 64–65, 70, 77
biggest 65
parts of 65
rocket 78–79
fuel 78
oxidizer 78, 79
ENIAC 24

F

Facebook 25, 27, 28, 29
Fanuc S420i robot 40
Farmville game 28
FBI 35
Ferrari, Enzo 69
Ferrari F40 69
fibre-optic cable 26
files 26
Flex-Foot Cheetah prosthetic leg 97
Flight Simulator 1.0 game 44
Flyer aeroplane 74
force 64, 65, 74, 78
drag 74
thrust 65, 74–75, 76–77, 78–79
Ford, Henry 68
fossil fuel 102
fridge, smart 93
Friese-Green, William 53
fuel 64, 66–67, 68, 78

G

Galileo satellite 28
Gamecube games console 44
gamepad 46, 47
iControlPad 47
game 23, 26, 28, 44–45, 46–47, 50
action 44
Angry Birds 46

PHOTOGRAPHY

1: Kulka/Corbis; 2–3: Maximilien Brice, CERN/Science Photo Library; 4cl: Science and Society/SuperStock; 6: Lockheed Martin Corporation; 7l: Kiyoshi Ota/X02055/Reuters/Corbis; 7cl: Bettmann/Corbis; 7cr: NASA; 7r: FLPA/Robin Chittenden/age fotostock; 8–9: Mona Lisa Production/Photo Researchers, Inc.; 10–11: NASA; 12c: B&C Alexander/Photo Researchers, Inc.; 12r: Kiyoshi Ota/X02055/Reuters/Corbis; 14tr: Ted Soqui/Corbis; 14bl: Nokia; 14bcl: Getty Images; 14bcr: Bloomberg via Getty Images; 14br: Science and Society/SuperStock; 15 (valve): Leif Norman/iStockphoto; 15 (transistor): Alexander Khromtsov/iStockphoto; 15 (microchip): alxpin/iStockphoto; 15bl: Science and Society/SuperStock; 15bc: Scott Aiken/Rex USA; 15br: LG; 16–17: Andrew Brookes/Corbis; 18–19 (MacBook Pro): Scholastic; 19tl: Rebelpilot/Flickr/Wikipedia; 19tc: iStockphoto; 20ct: iStockphoto; 23 (app icons): iStockphoto; 24tc: Science Source/Photo Researchers, Inc.; 24tr, 24b: Science Museum/Science & Society Picture Library; 25tl: Deborah Feingold/Corbis; 25tc: Peter Menzel/Photo Researchers, Inc.; 25tr: Mike Agliolo/Photo Researchers, Inc.; 25bl: Hank Morgan/Photo Researchers, Inc.; 25br: PSL Images/Alamy; 26–27 (Microsoft data center): Richard Duval/Microsoft; 26bl, 26br, 27bl: iStockphoto; 27br: Spanish Facebook; 30tl: Friedrich Saurer/Photo Researchers, Inc.; 30–31 (shark): iStockphoto; 31tr: Pixellover RM 10/Alamy; 31cr: Rafael Macia/Photo Researchers, Inc.; 31br: B&C Alexander/Photo Researchers, Inc.; 32–33 (Large Hadron Collider), 33bl: CERN; 33cr: Thierry Berrod, Mona Lisa Production/Photo Researchers, Inc.; 33br: Ali Yazdani & Daniel J. Hornbaker/Photo Researchers, Inc.; 34 (Goldfinger): AF archive/Alamy; 34cm: Wikipedia; 34cr: Corbis; 34br: Bettmann/Corbis; 35tl: SSPL via Getty Images; 35tr: Bettmann/Corbis; 35cl: Corbis; 35 (Gary Powers): Time & Life Pictures/Getty Images; 35 (memory stick): iStockphoto; 35 (Anna Chapman): Maxim Shipenkov/epa/Corbis; 35b: Getty Images; 36tl, 36 (arm tools), 36–37 (PackBot): iRobot; 37tr: AF archive/Alamy; 38–39: Kiyoshi Ota/X02055/Reuters/Corbis; 40tl: iStockphoto; 40tr: Science Source/Photo Researchers, Inc.; 40cl: John Zich/zrImages/Corbis; 40bl: David Vaughan/Photo Researchers, Inc.; 40br: Gostai, Inc.; 41: Sam Ogden/Photo Researchers, Inc.; 42l: AF archive/Alamy; 42c: Six Flags, Inc.; 44tl: Science and Society/SuperStock; 44tr: peter jordan/Alamy; 44bl: Science and Society/SuperStock; 44bc: Ralf-Finn Hestoft/Corbis; 44br: ArcadeImages/Alamy; 45tl: Haruyoshi Yamaguchi/Corbis; 45tr: Lightly Salted/Alamy; 45bl: Reuters/Corbis; 45bc: David Lee/Alamy; 45br: Oliver Berg/dpa/Corbis; 46tl, 46tr, 46 (Angry Birds on tablet), 46 (Angry Birds on phone): iStockphoto; 46cm: Bandai Namco Games; 46cr: Nintendo; 47tl: Lightly Salted/Alamy; 47tc: iStockphoto; 47tr: iControlPad; 47cl: Nintendo; 47cm: Microsoft Xbox; 47cr: iControlPad; 48tl: iStockphoto; 50–51 (CAVE): Teesside University; 52–53 (audience): Bettmann/Corbis; 53cr: AF archive/Alamy; 53br: Pascal Goetgheluck/Photo Researchers, Inc.; 54l, 55br: iStockphoto; 56tl: Tim Mosenfelder/Corbis; 58tl: Gamma-Rapho via Getty Images; 58tr: Getty Images; 58c: Robert Cianflone/Getty Images; 58bl: Six Flags Great Adventure/Splash/Newscom; 58br: Ahmad Yusni/epa/Corbis; 59: Sinibomb Images/Alamy; 59b: travelibUK/Alamy; 60–61: Six Flags, Inc.; 62l: AFP/Getty Images; 62c: NASA; 62tr: Keith Kent/Science Photo Library; 64–65 (Boeing): Grégoire Delatte; 66tl: Carnundrum/Alamy; 67cr: Transtock/SuperStock; 68tl: Motoring Picture Library/Alamy; 68tr: John Cairns/Alamy; 68bl: Omikron/Photo Researchers, Inc.; 68br: David Woods/Corbis; 69tl: PhotoStock10/Shutterstock; 69tr: Getty Images; 69bl: Microvision; 69br: izmostock/Alamy; 70tl: NASA Archive/Alamy; 70tr: ZUMA Press/Newscom; 70c: Edwards Air Force Base; 70bl: Tony Watson/Alamy; 70br: A kal fj/APimages; 71: Eric Risberg/APimages; 71br: Richard Meredith Hardy/RexUSA; 72–73: f1h2o, inc; 74cl: Tristar Photos/Alamy; 74bl: Simon Price/Alamy; 75: Richard Cooke/Alamy; 75br: NASA Ames Research Center/Photo Researchers, Inc.; 76–77 (WaveRunner): Gerald Julien/Getty Images; 77tl: Skyscan/Photo Researchers, Inc.; 77br: National Geographic Image Collection/Alamy; 78–79 (Endeavour): NASA; 79 (Saturn V): Friedrich Saurer/Photo Researchers, Inc.; 79 (Long March): China Great Wall Industry Corporation/Photo Researchers, Inc.; 79 (space shuttle): Photo Researchers, Inc.; 79 (Ariane 5): Reuters/Corbis; 79 (Soyuz-FG): NASA/Photo Researchers, Inc.; 80–81 (all), 82–83 (International Space Station), 83cr, 83br: NASA; 84l: Photo Researchers, Inc.; 84c: Science and Society/SuperStock; 86tl: SuperStock/Getty Images; 86bl, 87tr, 87br: iStockphoto; 88–89: Joe Fox/Alamy; 92tl: Nik Wheeler/Corbis; 92tr: Science and Society/SuperStock; 92bl: SSPL via Getty Images; 92br: Science and Society/SuperStock; 93tl: David Wooley/Getty Images; 93tr: Science and Society/SuperStock; 93bl: Comstock/Getty Images; 93br: Getty Images; 94tl: iStockphoto; 95tr: Alfred Pasieka/Photo Researchers, Inc.; 95br: Gustoimages/Photo Researchers, Inc.; 96tr: Shawn Hempel/Shutterstock; 96cl: Photos 12/Alamy; 96cr: James King-Holmes/Photo Researchers, Inc.; 96br: i-limb ultra; 96–97 (body): Science Picture Company; 97cl: Abiomed; 97 (Flex-Foot): Össur; 97 (Oscar Pistorius): Eric Lalmand/epa/Corbis; 97 (hip joint): Alexander Tsiaras/Photo Researchers, Inc.; 97br: Coneyl Jay/Photo Researchers, Inc.; 98–99: Greenbird, Inc.; 100–101 (wind farm): FLPA/Robin Chittenden/age fotostock; 100tl: Sunpix Travel/Alamy; 101tl: iStockphoto; 101tcl: Martin Bond/Photo Researchers, Inc.; 101tcr: Tom McHugh/Photo Researchers, Inc.; 101tr: Helix Wind; 101c: Martin Bond/Photo Researchers, Inc.; 102tl: Planet Solar SA, Inc.; 102tr: Clynt Garnham Renewable Energy/Alamy; 102cr: Voltaic, Inc.; 102bl, 102br: Quant, Inc.; 103b: Photo Researchers, Inc.; 104–105: LAVA (Laboratory for Visionary Architecture); 104br: Fosters & Partners, London; 108: Hugh Threlfall/Alamy.

ARTWORK

12l, 20–21 (smartphone), 42r, 48–49 (camcorder), 56–57 (guitar), 66–67 (car), 84r, 86–87 (bike), 94–95 (shoe): Tim Loughhead/Precision Illustration; all other artwork: Scholastic.

COVER

Front cover: (tablet surrounding icons) Hbas/Shutterstock; (icons) Lana Rinck/Shutterstock and iStockphoto; (finger) Discpicture/Shutterstock. Back cover: (robot hand) iStockphoto; (handheld electronic game) Kevork Djansezian/Getty Images; (computer screen) Manaemedia/Dreamstime.

Credits and acknowledgement